Henry Bernstein

The Targum of Onkelos to Genesis

Henry Bernstein

The Targum of Onkelos to Genesis

ISBN/EAN: 9783337198237

Printed in Europe, USA, Canada, Australia, Japan

Cover: Foto ©Lupo / pixelio.de

More available books at **www.hansebooks.com**

THE TARGUM

OF

ONKELOS TO GENESIS

A CRITICAL ENQUIRY

INTO THE VALUE OF THE TEXT EXHIBITED BY YEMEN MSS.
COMPARED WITH THAT OF THE EUROPEAN RECENSION

TOGETHER WITH

SOME SPECIMEN CHAPTERS OF THE ORIENTAL TEXT

BY

HENRY BARNSTEIN. Ph. D.

LONDON 1896
DAVID NUTT
270-271 STRAND.

W. DRUGULIN
LEIPZIG.

DEDICATED

TO

MY REVERED TEACHER AND FRIEND

THE REV. DR. M. GASTER

to whom I owe an everlasting debt of gratitude for the instruction received at his hands and the constant interest he has shown in my welfare.

PREFACE.

THE purpose of this enquiry is to critically investigate the recension of the Targum of Onkelos preserved in the Yemen Mss. and to establish a comparison between these Mss. and the Western or European texts, which are at present best represented by Berliner's recent edition. Berliner did not avail himself, however, of these Eastern Mss. and his edition is therefore, to a certain extent, inadequate and can hardly be accepted as final. In order to establish a critical edition this enquiry goes into minute details of grammar, differences of vocalization and orthography, additions and omissions, interchange of particles and variant readings. Part I contains the general outlines of this research and the results arrived at. Part II shows the more detailed comparison and lists of examples, following the text of the Bible, chapter and verse. The investigation concludes with a few specimen chapters of the Targum text, according to the version given by the Yemen Mss. It will probably reflect the original Palestinian form. Instead of making an index I have given a detailed Table of Contents. It is my fervent hope that this humble effort may be appreciated by students of the Bible and may give an incentive to the true appreciation of the work of Onkelos.

H. B.

CONTENTS.

PART I.

CHAPTER I. *History of the Text* . . . . pp. 1—3.
1) Importance of the Translation (1).—2) Where it originated (2).—Travels (2).—3) Effects of travels upon text (2).—Present texts (2).

CHAPTER II. *Onkelos and his Translation* . . pp. 3—5.
1) Approximate date of work (3).—2) Character of his Targum (4).—3) Halachic and Haggadic elements (4).—4) Public recital of Targum (5).

CHAPTER III. *Importance of the Yemen Mss.* pp. 6—11.
1) Hitherto their linguistic character alone studied (6).—2) Origin of Superlinear vocalization (6).—3) Targum never neglected in Palestine (8).—4) The Babylonian Redaction (9).—5) Differences of Yemen Mss. (10). 6) They represent the original Palestinian version (10).—7) Object of Investigation (10).

CHAPTER IV. *Description of Mss.* . . . . pp. 11—13.

CHAPTER V. *Superlinear Vocalization* . . . pp. 13—17.
1) Signs employed in this system (13). — 2) Appropriate to Aramaic (14).—3) Origin of system (14).—4) Absence of Segol (15; 45).[a]—5) Absence of Šewa Compositum (15; 45—46).—6) No sign for Šewa Quiescens (16).—7) No sign for Dageš or Rafe (16).—8) Approach to Biblical Aramaic and Syriac (17).—9) Agreement with Biblical Aramaic (17).

CHAPTER VI. *Differences of Vocalization* . . pp. 18—25.
1) Less frequent use of vowel letters (18).—2) Superlinear system etymologically more correct (18).—3) Interchange of vowels. Western texts Pataḥ=Yemen Qameṣ (18—19; 46); *a.* Monosyllabic words and particles.

(*a*) Second number in brackets refers to the pages of the corresponding portion in Part II.

b. 3rd Per. Sin. Pret. Peal of ו״י.   *c.* 3rd. Per. Sin. Pret. Peal of Mediae Geminatae. *d.* Present Participle. *e.* 3rd Sin. Pret. Feminine. *f.* Suffix of 2nd Per. Sin. *g.* Miscellaneous words. Western Qameṣ = Yemen Pataḥ (19; 47). *a.* Suffix of 3rd Per. Sin. Fem. *b.* Vowel of 2nd Radical of Verb. *c.* Little change in Pause. *d.* Vowel before Suffixes ־ְ and נָ. *e.* Other instances.—4) Western Ṣere = Yemen Ḥireq (19; 47), Western Ḥireq = Yemen Ṣere (19; 47,.—5) Western Šureq = Yemen Ḥolem (20; 47). Western Ḥolem = Yemen Šureq (20; 48).—6) The vowel of the Imperfect (20; 48).— 7) Various interchanges (21; 48). *a.* West. Ḥireq = Yemen Pataḥ. *b.* West. Pataḥ = Yem. Ḥireq. *c.* West. Ṣere = Yem. Pataḥ. *d.* West. Pataḥ = Yem. Ṣere. *e.* West. Pataḥ = Yem. Ḥolem. *f.* West. Ḥolem = Yem. Ṣere. *g.* West. Ṣere = Yem. Ḥolem. *h.* West. Šureq = Yem. Ḥireq. *i.* West. Ḥolem = Yem. Qameṣ. *j.* West. Šureq = Yem. Qameṣ. *k.* West. Pataḥ = Yem. Ṣere. *l.* West. Pataḥ = Yem. Šureq.—8) Interchange of Vowels and Šewa (22; 48—49). *a.* West. Pataḥ = Yem. Šewa. *b.* West. Qameṣ = Yem. Šewa. *c.* West. Ṣere = Yem. Šewa. *d.* West. Šewa = Yem. Ṣere. *e.* West. Ḥireq = Yem. Šewa.—9) The Yemenite Pronunciation (22).—10) General results (25).

CHAPTER VII. *Variations in orthography.*   pp. 25—28; 49—53.

a. Dialectical Variations. *b.* Use of vowel change to distinguish similar words. *c.* 3rd Pers. Plu. of לא in ו. *d.* Interchange of letters. *e.* Other changes. *f.* בשון מריבים. *g.* קרא ותרגים. *h.* Marginal readings. *i.* Agreement of Mss. with Nehardean Tradition.

CHAPTER VIII. *Grammatical Variations* . . pp. 28—35.

1) The Noun (28—33; 53—57). *a.* State. α. Absolute and Emphatic. β. Absolute and Construct. *b.* Number. *c.* Gender.— 2) The Verb (33—35; 57—60). *a.* The Conjugations. α. Peal and Pael. β. Peal and Afel. γ. Peal and Etpeel, Etpaal or Ettafal. δ. Pael and Afel. ε. Etpeel and Etpaal. *b.* The Tenses. α. Perfect and Imperfect. β. Perfect and (Participle) Present. γ. Imperfect and (Participle) Present. *c.* Other Differences.

CHAPTER IX. *Other Variations* . . . . . pp. 35—39.

1) How additions and omissions may be accounted for (35—36).— 2) Additions (36—37; 60—62).—3) Omissions (37—38; 62).— 4) Contractions (38).—5) Interchange of Prepositions and other Particles (38—39; 62—65) [Hebraisms 65].—6) Variations in Suffix (39).

CHAPTER X. *Exegetical Variations*   pp. 39—42: 66—77.

PART II.

CHAPTER I. *Remarks upon the words:*
איתיליד; קביל; קדם; בל; יה . . pp. 43—45.

CHAPTER II. *Examples of the rules contained in Part I.*
pp. 45—77.

CHAPTER III. *Specimen Chapters* . . . . pp. 78—end.
Introductory remarks (78). Genesis XVII (79). XXVI (81). XXXI (85). XLI (92).

LIST OF ABBREVIATIONS.

A = Ms. Codex Montefiore. No. 502.
B = ,, ,, ,, ,, 508.
C = ,, Brit. Museum. Or. No. 2363.
D = ,, Codex Gaster. No. 2.
B. = Berliner's Targum Onkelos (Berlin 1884).
Bbl. = Babylonian.
Bib. Aram. = Biblical Aramaic.
D. = Dageš.
Hag. = Haggadic.
Hal. = Halachic.
Ḥ. = Ḥireq.
Ḥt. = Ḥatef.
Ḥo. = Ḥolem.
L. = Levy's Chaldäisches Wörterbuch (Leipzig 1866).
Luz. = Luzzatto's Philoxenos (Vienna 1830).
O. = Onkelos.
P. = Patah.
Plst. = Palestinian.
Q. = Qameṣ.
R. = Rafe.
S. = Segol.
Ṣ. = Šureq.
Ṣ. = Ṣere.
Še. = Šewa.
Spl. = Superlinear.
Sbl. = Sublinear.
Trg. = Targum.

I. HISTORY OF THE TEXT.

1. It is universally acknowledged that of all the Translations of the Bible that bearing the name of Onkelos enjoyed the greatest veneration from very ancient times; because it rests upon the Exegesis of the Tanaim, and is considered to represent the original traditional Interpretation.

Its sanctity was enhanced when the Amoraim invested it with great authority by making it an official decree that it should be publicly read in the Synagogue side by side with the Hebrew original.

The neglect of this Rabbinical decree was in later times greatly blamed by some of the Geonim. This neglect of the Targum was most noticeable among the Jews living in arabic-speaking countries, after the arabic language had supplanted the Aramaic as the Jewish vernacular. Among other authorities who have blamed the Jews for their laxity in carrying out the principle of שנים מקרא ואחד תרגום the names of Jehuda b. Qoreis, Samuel Hanagid and the Geonim Natronai and Hai stand out most prominently.

Their admonitions had a salutary effect for throughout the middle ages and at the present time this precept is strictly adhered to, and this accounts for the veneration in which it is held by the Jews — a veneration which, it may be added, is shared by all students of Holy Writ, on account of the light which this translation throws upon many obscure passages in the Bible, as well as for its intrinsic merits[1].

---

[1] Cf. Delitzsch „Zur Geschichte der jüdischen Poesie". Leipzig 1836, pp. 27 and 135.

2. The Targum originated in Palestine, but was subsequently transplanted to Babylon where it enjoyed great esteem, coming, as it did from the Holy Land. Similarly we find the study of the Calendar and the Ritual pursued with great zest in Babylon, both of which are products of Palestinian learning. In Babylon, as we shall see more clearly presently, a fresh redaction of the text was made, which differed in many respects, from the original Plst. Version.

From Babylon the Trg. travelled to Europe, first to Italy and then to Germany and Northern France, and also to Spain and Provence.

3. In the course of its travels, the text of the Trg. became more and more corrupt. Some time[1] after its arrival in Europe the original Spl. vocalization was exchanged for the Sbl. system which was used for the Hebrew language, a change which had the most pernicious effect upon the text. The evil was aggravated by the ignorance of the European scribes who inserted marginal glosses in the text and heaped errors upon errors until the text of the Trg. became in an all-but-hopeless condition.

4. The result of this is seen in the texts which are in common use to-day. These are far from perfect. Various expedients have been tried from time to time to improve the text with but indifferent success, the reason being that all the would-be amenders started from an incorrect standpoint. They all assumed that the European copies were based upon the original text, whereas they originate from the Bbl. Redaction. Buxtorf wished to remodel the text according to Bibl. Aram., quite ignoring the fact that a long time had elapsed between the Aramaic of the Bible and that of the Trg. and that the Trg. was composed under entirely different circumstances, and for an entirely different purpose.

Lagarde thought he would be serving the interests of

---

[1] At the beginning of the 12th century by Nathan B. Machir of Ancona, according to an epigraph of the Codex 12 of de Rossi v. Berliner „Targum Onkelos". Berlin 1884, Vol. II, p. 134.

science in the best way by omitting the vowel-signs and confining his attention to establishing a correct and critical consonantal text, but, it must be remarked, he did not even attain this ideal.

Berliner's edition of the Targum[1], (B.) which is a reprint of the Sabionetta edition of 1554 suffers for the same reason as all other European Editions. His sources are all European MSS. none of which exhibit the original text but the subsequent Babyl. redaction. It is undoubtedly superior to any of its predecessors, besides which the edition is invaluable containing as it does the products of a life-study and embodying the ripe results of all B.'s predecessors in the same branch of learning. Before proceeding to the investigation how our Trg. texts may be improved by reference to MSS. unknown to B. and hitherto all-but-neglected and which will serve as basis for our own investigations it is necessary to know something about O., his time and the general character of his translation of the Pentateuch.

II. ONKELOS AND HIS TRANSLATION.

1. As to the date of this translation much difference of opinion has existed. Frankel[2] and Geiger[3] place its date in the time of the later Talmudists, but by observing certain characteristics of the translation B. has fixed the time as contemporaneous with or immediately following the time of R. ʿAqiba; second half of the second century. He bases this opinion upon the Targumist's consistent avoidance of anthropomorphisms (which is also a characteristic of the LXX), the little necessity felt for aramaicising Greek words —these words being *au courant* in the original Greek in ʿAqiba's time—and the Targumic embodiment of ʿAqiba's hal. and hag. principles[4].

---

[1] Berlin: 1884.   [2] „Zu dem Targum der Propheten". Breslau 1872, p. 9.   [3] Urschrift und die Übersetzungen der Bibel. Breslau 1857, p. 164.   [4] l. c. pp. 102—108. Cf. also Zunz "Gottesd. Vort." Frankfort 1892, p. 132.

2. As regards the character of this Translation, this is described with great clearness and minuteness by B.[1] Our Trg. is neither too literal nor too free; it shows a remarkable agreement with the Massoretic Text[2]; it always follows the Qerē leaving the Ketib unnoticed[3] a characteristic which is also noticeable in a MS. of Daniel with Spl. vocalization which came under my notice, and the importance of which will be considered in chapter VIII. The Targumist omits certain pleonasms which are to be found in the Hebrew text[4], he occasionally endeavours to imitate the sound of the original text[5], employs a rich store of synonyms, occasionally makes use of circumlocution and simplifies figurative expressions. Both the Tetragrammaton and אלהים are rendered יי[6], which was written ייי (until this was taken as a sign for the Trinity), of which various modifications, such as ייי, ייד, ייד are found. The reason of the Targumist's dislike of the word אלהים is found in the employment of this word for strange gods[7]. When יי אלהים occur together, the Targumist must naturally reproduce them as they occur in the Hebrew text.

3. According to Rapoport[8], where we have a law which applies to the administration of justice the Targumist renders literally, but where a command occurs which affects each individual member of the community, the traditional explanation is given. But so many exceptions to this rule are to be found, that it must be rejected, and that given by Adler[9] substituted for it. This rule runs thus—Whenever the Targumist has to meet the contradictory views of Sectarians, or in those cases wherein the people have not yet attained a complete knowledge of

[1] pp. 206—224 l. c. [2] l. c. p. 207. [3] l. c. p. 209. [4] l. c. p. 210. [5] l. c. p. 211. [6] l. c. p. 223. [7] That this is not always the case may be seen from Exodus 12, 12 where אלהי מצרים is rendered טעות מצראי. [8] In Kerem Ḥ'emed V, 223 and VI, 220 also in דבר משאת שלום (Prague: 1861) p. 11. [9] In the Introduction to his נתינה לגר Wilna: 1874.

the tradition, or when the Tanaim themselves differ upon the point in question, the Targumist gives the better of the two traditions, but where the tradition is unassailable he renders literally [1]. Singer, however, says we can lay down no general rule, but O. employs the Halacha in his translation where a literal rendering would remain obscure [2].

4. Great care was taken to ensure the correct recital of the Trg., this being especially the case with the Trg. of the Pentateuch [3]. A verse was given out by the Reader in Hebrew, which was immediately followed by its Aramaic translation rendered by the Meturgeman. More laxity was allowed with the recital of the Prophets, in which three verses were taken together before the Meturgeman recited their translation [4]. Both Reader and Meturgeman had to preserve a reverential demeanour, in virtue of the solemn office which they held [5]. As, however, a standard official translation had not then yet appeared, opportunity was given to the Meturgemanim to insert their own interpretation of the text. This privilege was occasionally abused and we find some of the Meturgemanim blamed by the Rabbis [6] on this account. The writing down of the Trg.—just as that of the Mišna—was at first prohibited [7], but this prohibition only applied to the writing down for the purpose of public reading, but private copies could be held by the scribes for their own use.

---

[1] B. l. c. pp. 224—225. [2] Singer: „Onkelos und das Verhältniss seines Targums zur Halacha". Halle 1881. [3] B. l. c. p. 84. [4] Cf. Mišna. Megillah IV, 4 and Talmud. Bab. Tr. Megillah 24 a. [5] Cf. Tur, Oraḥ Ḥayyim ch. 145 and Maimonides הלכ׳ תפלה XII, 11. In Tal. Bab. Tr. Megillah Cap. III. R. Nissim quotes a Jerusalemitan Talmud as the origin of this custom. [6] Cf. Talmud of Babylon Tr. Megillah 23 b and 24 a. [7] Cf. Talm. Jer. Tr. Megillah IV, 1 and Talmud Bab. Sabbath 115 a. v. Zunz. l. c. p. 65.

III. IMPORTANCE OF THE YEMEN MSS.

1. It is strange that hitherto only European MSS. have been studied in connection with the Trg. Since then however a number of Targum MSS. have come to Europe from South Arabia but have received little attention; scholars having regarded them of linguistic importance only. In this way, one of them (which I shall subsequently call *C*) has been employed by B.[1], Merx[2] and Margoliouth[3].

2. At the outset of our investigation into the importance of these MSS. we must ask ourselves two questions.

Is it correct to call the Spl. system of vocalization the Babyl. system? Does the study of the Trg. in Babylon, or the redaction of a version of the Trg. in that country necessarily imply that its study was neglected in its mother-country, Palestine? Now the Spl. punctuation has been frequently described as the Babyl. system[4], a nomenclature which

---

[1] l. c. pp. 159—160.   [2] "Chrestomathia Targumica", Berlin 1888, pp. 68—103.   [3] On the Superlinear vocalization (Transactions of the 9th Congress of Orientalists II, London 1893), pp. 46—56.
[4] Thus Neubauer connects the Yemen Jews with Babylon in his article on "The Literature of the Jews in Yemen" (Jewish Quarterly Review III, pp. 604—622). Speaking of the epitaphs which have been discovered in Yemen, Neubauer says (p. 608): "These epitaphs, dated according to the era of the contracts point to an acquaintance with the Babylonian schools, for the Italian early epitaphs date from the era of the destruction of the 2nd Temple and later on bear, in addition, the era of the creation. The Jews of Yemen continue up to the present day to date from the era of the contracts, using Aramaic formulae, which point more to Babylonia than to Palestine. Moreover, the use of superlinear vowel-points (usually called Assyrian Punctuation) in the pointed Hebrew Texts written in Yemen would argue their connection with the Eastern Massoretic Schools rather than with the Palestinian one at Tiberias". But Margoliouth is not at all certain of the Bbl. origin of the Spl. vocalization. "The theory which identifies the originators of the superlinear punctuation with the Masoretic Schools of the מדנחאי or "Easterns" rests partly on an epigraph in he Parmese Codex de Rossi 12 of A. D. 1311, and partly—or rather

is also employed by B., but, as far as can be observed, no proofs have yet been given to show its Bbl. origin[1]. B.[2] says: "it is doubtful when the vowel-signs were first added but probably they were added in Babylon, in which country the peculiar Spl. punctuation was in use". No reason is advanced why we should make this assumption. Then why assume that they were added in Babylon? Is it not just as likely that they were originally written in Palestine and came over to Babylon with the Trg. text?

This seems the more probable after Nöldeke's assertion[3] that "the authoritative Targum although redacted in Babylon

chiefly—on the internal evidence afforded by the readings and marginal rubrics of the Codex Babylonicus" (l. c. p. 51). But he proceeds to point out that this is a very flimsy foundation for the origin of the Spl. system. How can we trust a single scribe of the 14th century whilst the contemporaries of the originators of this system are silent on the subject. Margoliouth especially singles out Saadia and points out how inexplicable his silence would be were the superlinear system of Bbl. origin. As for the internal evidence from the Codex Babylonicus it must be remembered that this MS. does not exhibit the primitive Spl. system, but shows the Spl. punctuation in a highly composite and developed form which would naturally approach the Eastern or Bbl. forms of that Masoretic School. Hence it is hardly fair to argue from this MS. to prove the Bbl. origin. Margoliouth also refutes various other theories which have been set up to prove the origin of this system, but his own theory that this system represents a mixed nestorian-jacobite punctuation appears to be very forced, and is more than improbable if we are to admit this system to be of Palestinian origin. Cf. Seligsohn pp. 12, 19, 32.

[1] Likewise Dalman: „Zwar ist die superlineare Vokalisation der von dort neuerlich nach Europa gekomenen Targumhandschriften keineswegs als aramäische Wiedergabe palästinischer Aussprache des Aramäischen anzusehen. Vielmehr wird sie einer in Babylonien gelehrten schulmässigen Behandlung des Onkelostargums entstammen, der gegenüber der Konsonantentext der sog. jerusalemischen Targume öfters eine ältere und urwüchsigere Form des Onkelostextes repräsentiert" (Grammatik des jüdisch-palästinischen Aramäisch, Leipzig 1894, I, p. V—VI). [2] l. c. p. 131. [3] Th. Nöldeke, Mandäische Grammatik. Halle 1875. Introduction p. V.

exhibits a dialect whose fundamental characteristics are Palestinian.

For the present then, the system should be called the Superlinear (Spl.) system, without defining it further as either Bbl. or Plst. we shall see further on in chapter V how much more appropriate this system is to the Aramaic language than the Sbl. system now in use.

3. B.[1] states that for various reasons but principally through the decay of the Plst. schools, the Trg. left its native country and its study was transferred to Babylon. But are we sure that the Trg. ever left Palestine or that its study was neglected by the Jews of the Holy Land? May it not have travelled to Babylon—just as the Calendar and Ritual did—and yet have been continued in Palestine? It is true that the Jews of Palestine were greatly harassed in their studies by political troubles which interfered with their liberty and yet we know that they were always the great leaders of the study of the Bible, a fact which the Massora—that invaluable guide to the correct Text of our Hebrew Bible—and the various Midrašim bear witness to.

Now we know that both the Massora and the Midrasim hail from Palestine. Again, the Jerusalem Trg. which has come down to us, although differing in character from the Trg. of O., shows at least that the study of the Trg. was pursued in Palestine. Now this Jerusalem Trg. is entirely hagadic in character, may we not then assume that side by side with this hag. Trg. there existed a literal Trg., the same version, in fact, which was transferred to Babylon? Just as Palestine produced two such varied studies as those of the Massora and Midraš, it is probable that the two Recensions of the Trg.—the literal and the hag.—existed in this country side by side. This will perhaps be seen more clearly after it will be shown that Yemen MSS. appear to contain the original Plst. text.

[1] l. c. p. 108.

4. The natural result of the attention bestowed upon the Trg. in Babylon is seen in that redaction of the text which although adhering to the original version to a great extent must have inevitably become somewhat corrupted in its language in course of time, in spite of the efforts of the Rabbis of the time to preserve the text intact by placing the stamp of their authority upon it. As texts became multiplied more mistakes must have gradually crept in. As the words were also, in all probability, differently pronounced in Babylon, their orthography became changed, and the original vocalization must have been at least considerably modified. Another tendency became noticeable in the substitution of hag. explanations in the place of the original literal rendering. In time a reaction set in in favour of the original Plst. Version; and this movement is represented by the so-called Nehardean tradition, in contradistinction to the tradition of Sura, which is substantially represented by the text which we find to-day in our European editions. When the Trg. came to Europe it was then punctuated in the original Spl. vocalization which it had probably received in Palestine. Some time after its arrival[1], this Spl. vocalization was altered in favour of the Sbl. system in use with the Hebrew text. This inevitably led to great confusion[2], for the Trg. text had already undergone considerable modifications after its arrival in Babylon, and now another alteration taking place which practically involved the rewriting of the text in its entirety the result can easily be imagined. As copies were increased in Europe the evil became magnified and was greatly aggravated by the ignorance shown by the scribes, of the Aramaic language; the result of all this we have already seen in the various devices made by scholars to amend the corrupt text. These were all unsuccesful because the scholars depended upon the Babyl. recension

---

[1] v. B. l. c. p. 134. [2] "Our editions are greatly neglected, whilst old editions and MSS. have superior readings". (A. Geiger: Nachgelassene Schriften, Vol. 4, Berlin 1876, p. 104.)

which must have been a considerable modification of the Plst. original.

5. Of late years a rich store of treasure has been brought to light by the discovery of MSS. of the Trg. from Yemen most of which are punctuated with the Spl. vocalization, a fact which in itself invites the student to their study if only from a linguistic point of view. On examining these MSS. more closely most far-reaching and profound differences are to be found. These variations occur not only in the vocalization, pronunciation and orthography but also in the exegesis of the text itself, especially in the interpretation of several important hag. and poetical passages, in which cases the usual hag. interpretation is replaced by a literal translation.[1]

What then do all these peculiar facts point to? It is unlikely that the Jews of Yemen had a peculiar tradition of their own although we know that they settled in Southern Arabia at a very early period. "Certain it is that centuries before Mohammed there were powerful Jewish communities in North Arabia as well as in South Arabia or Yemen"[2].

6. The various differences which are noticeable in these Trg. MSS. induce one to believe that they represent the original Plst. text. The changes in vocalization, pronunciation and orthography remind us—as will be shown in chapters V to VIII—of the Bib. Aram. and Syriac grammatical forms and approximate more closely to the Nehardean tradition, or we may perhaps call it the Nehardean recension. The preference shown for a literal translation may be accounted for by observing that the Plst. Jews had another Trg. which is entirely hag. in tendency.

7. The object, then, of this investigation is to endeavour

---

[1] Geiger although ascribing a Babylonian origin to the Targum of Onkelos points out that its character is literality, which he regards as a later protest against the fanciful interpretations of the earlier exegetists. l. c. vol. 4, p. 104.   [2] v. Neubauer l. c. p. 605.

to show the true character of the original Trg. of O. and so pave the way for a critical edition of that Trg. I will now deal separately with each of the points enumerated above, and show in how far these characteristics strengthen our views as to the original and Plst. character of the Trg. of these MSS. But before entering into the examination of these MSS., a short description of those I have made use of, may be now given.

IV. THE YEMEN MSS.

1. Codex Montefiore, No. 502; which I call *A* is peculiar in having a Sublinear vocalization for the Aramaic as well as for the Hebrew text, which may perhaps be regarded as an unsuccesful attempt on the part of the scribe to bring the two systems of vocalization into harmony with each other. It also differs from the other MSS. in having the Hebrew text in large square characters in the middle of the page, whilst the Trg. and Arabic translation are placed on the sides and the commentary of Raši below. It consists of 133 folios and extends till the end of Exodus. The writing is bold, square and pointed; and the paper stout and dark. It is probably of the 18th century and is written throughout in one hand (except the marginal notes). The quires consist of 7 leaves, but nearly every leaf has the custos at the bottom. The number of lines in each page, both in the Hebrew text, and in the Aramaic and Arabic translations at the sides, naturally varies according to the length of the commentary of Raši below, but the average number is 19 lines for the Hebrew text, 30 for the translations and about 8 for the commentary. The Hebrew text has an average of 8 words to the line. There are no massoretic directions except that at the end of every Paraša the number of verses contained in that portion is given with a mnemonic. It is one of the characteristics of Eastern MSS.

that they have little or no illuminations, and all these MSS. (except *C*) have only an ornamental figure on the margin at the end of every Paraša.

2. Codex Montefiore, No. 508. I call this MS. *B*. This is a remarkably fine and clear MS. and will be frequently found to be valuable in retaining the original literal rendering, whilst an haggadic interpretation is inserted on the margin. It consists of 159 folios, 4 leaves making a quire; the custos, being given at irregular intervals, an average of 24 lines to a page and 10 words to a line. Thick, oriental paper and the oldest part in bold and round hand. It is unfortunately in a very imperfect condition and is written in no less than four distinct handwritings, of which the third and fourth appear to be quite modern. The oldest hand extends from f. 3—87, 98—102 and 104—110 and is Spl. throughout, both Hebrew and Aramaic, it probably dates from the 16th or 17th century; the second hand (f. 78—79, 103 and 111—155), has the Sbl. vocalization for the Hebrew and the Spl. for the Trg. It is less round and bold; and is perhaps of the 17th or 18th centuries, the third (f. 1—2, 156—159) is much more minute and is Sbl. throughout; probably 18th or 19th century. The fourth hand has added numerous marginal readings as well as Genesis 44, 10—15. Many verses in the second hand are left entirely unpunctuated. Again the only Massoretic note is the number of verses contained in each Paraša. The MS. extends till Exodus 24, 2. Each Hebrew verse is followed first by its Targum. and then by its Arabic translation.

3. *C* is the British Museum MS. Or. 2363 and has been fully described by Dr. Berliner[1].

4. *D* was placed at my disposal by the Rev. Dr. Gaster (Codex Heb. Gaster No. 2) and is the most perfect and reliable of all; scribes' errors being few and far between; and no sign being used either for Dag. or R. The paper is thinner

---

[1] l. c. pp. 132, 134 (Note 4), 137, 159 and 160.

than that of *A* or *B*, and the writing is beautifully clear and round; probably 17th century. It consists of 159 folios, written throughout in one hand and extends till the end of Exodus. There are about 27 lines to each page and about 14 words to each line. The MS. has been rebound, hence it is impossible to tell the quires, but every page has the custos. There are frequent marginal notes by a later hand; the only Massoretic notes being the number of verses at the end of every Paraša and the number of פסוחות and סתומות at the end of each Book. A note at the end informs us that the scribe's name was משה בן סעדיא בן יהודה; whilst a notice inside the original cover seems to point that the MS. was in somebody's possession in 1809. It runs דהוה הלת שני יובין לחושר (לחודש?) אדר ראשון שנת תרין אלפין ומא(ה) ועשרין וחד שנין לשט(רות). This points to the year 2121 of the Seleucidan era, corresponding to 1809 C. E. The last page is adorned with a cabalistic devise with a large figure of the Menorah, each branch of the candlestick having an appropriate scriptural quotation. Each verse is followed by its Trg. and then by its Arabic translation. All the MSS. are Folios and have been very much used.

V. THE SUPERLINEAR VOCALIZATION[1].

1. We will first consider the system of vocalization used in these MSS.

In the Spl. vocalization we have six vowel-signs which are written above the consonants. These are Qameṣ˘ (Q.), Pataḥ˘ (P.), Ṣere˘ (S.), Ḥireq˙ (H.), Ḥolem ˙ (Ho.) and Šureq ˙ (S.). Besides these signs a horizontal line represents the Šewa

---

[1] This system has only been lately discovered, being brought to light by the Karaite Rabbi Firkowitsh about 50 years ago. It represents the older system, since it is more simple and primitive than the sublinear system (cf. also the expression נקד על) and it is unusual to regress from a well developed to a primitive vocalisation.

Mobile and in *C* a slanting line ' indicates the Rafe sign. *A*, *B* and *C* also make occasional use of the Dag. point within the letter.

2. This system of punctuation is peculiarly appropriate to the Aramaic language. The inevitable Hebraisms which must occur in a text punctuated with vowel-signs which were taken direct from those in use in the Hebrew language are not noticeable in the Spl. system. As an example, we may take, the absence of any particuliar sign to represent the Ḥatef. This semi-vowel is unknown in the Aramaic language and in Biblical Aramaic it must have been taken from the Hebrew. It is remarkable that in a Bible MS. which I consulted in the British Museum (Or. 2374), the only words in Daniel and Ezra which seemed to have a particular sign for the Šewa compositum are קדם and קבל which are written thus קדם and קבל. This appropriateness of the Spl. system to Aramaic leads us to think that it was invented for the Aramaic language in Palestine as was suggested by Dr. Gaster in the course of his lectures at Montefiore College; and that it is, consequently, just as incorrect to apply the Spl. system to the Hebrew language—as some of the Yemen MSS. do—as it is to apply the Sbl. system to the Aramaic language.

3. Various suggestions have been made with respect to the origin of this system, but this is still a matter of conjecture. Strack[1] remarks "The so-called Babylonian or more accurately the Superlinear punctuation the vowel-signs of which are simplified forms of the matres lectionis א, ו and ״ and the detached accents of which usually have the shape of the letters with which their name begins was in use among the non-Palestinian Jews of Asia". But no proof for this statement is forthcoming. We have already noticed that Margoliouth[2] tries to prove that the system is of a mixed Nestorian-Jacobite character.

[1] "Einleitung in das alte Testament". Nördlingen 1888, p. 74.
[2] l. c. p. 47.

4. In the first place we must at once notice that the vowel-sign Segol is unknown in the Spl. system, other vowel-signs being substituted for it. In the Yemenite MSS. which Derenbourg saw and described in his "Manuel du Lecteur"[1] P. was invariably used for S.; but in the MSS. which I used S. is replaced by P., Ṣ. and even by Ḥ., the particular vowel being in most cases justifiable by reference to the word's etymology or by comparing the word in the cognate Semitic languages. This shows that the scribes must have been very careful in preserving the correct original orthography and is another argument in favour of the greater antiquity and authenticity of the Trg. as exhibited in the texts of the Yemen MSS.[2] A few Instances are given here[3], but detailed lists will be found in Part II.

S. is replaced by P. in בֵּיזֵי 2, 8, אִרֵי 11, 7. S. is replaced by Ṣ. in שׁוּבֵאַי 14, 2, בֵּלְבָּאֵ 25, 9. Very rarely by Ḥ.; e. g. in the word הֶדְיוֹט 28, 17 (Greek ἰδιώτης).

5. Besides having no S., the Spl. system of vocalization has no sign for Šewa Compositum. This sign—as has been previously remarked—is characteristic of the Hebrew and not of the Aramaic language[4].—In the MSS. it is usually replaced by Še. Mobile, or more rarely by Še. Quiescens or a Full Vowel. Še. Mobile replaces Ḥt.-P. in הִרֵי 1, 2.— It replaces Ḥt.-Q. in קֳדָם 4, 10 and Ḥt.-S. in אֱלָהִים 36, 11. Še. Quiescens replaces Ḥt.-P. in יַחֲזֵי 2, 10 and Ḥt.-S. in לְבִלְתִּי 17, 7. A full vowel is found in the MSS. where B. writes a Še. Compositum in such words as הִיא 29, 34.

Strange to say, Še. Compositum is found in a few isolated examples which have either crept into the MSS. by

---

[1] Journal Asiatique. Sixième Série. Tome XVI. No. 61. Paris 1870. [2] Cf. VI, 2. [3] In all examples which will be quoted, Berliner's edition of the Targum is the one referred to for the European readings, but the readings quoted are those given by the MSS [4] Cf. also the absence of any sign in Christian Palestinian Aramaic for Še. Compositum, Nöldeke, Beiträge zur Kenntniss der aramäiscenh Dialecte. ZDMG. XXII, p. 507.

error, or, are exactly taken as they were found in the Hebrew text; the majority of these instances being Proper Names. A and D both write לְקׇבֵּל 33, 18 (the other 2 MSS. B and C, more consistently לׇקֳבֵל)¹.

6. A third sign which is not represented in the Spl. vocalization is the Še. Quiescens; which is also wanting in Syriac.

7. The Spl. punctuation as originally written had no sign either for D. or R. and there is no doubt that originally the Aramaic language had no signs to indicate the harder or softer pronunciation of the letters בגדכפת. Margoliouth remarks "The oldest-known MSS. only use the D. in the Hebrew, but not in the Trg., a fact which seems to show that the D. is not a part of the Spl. system as such², but that it was adopted into the text from the other system of Hebrew punctuation, which one may fitly call the Sbl. vowel-system. Or. 2363 has a special sign for the רפי over the letters בגדכפת but in later MSS. in which the Dg. is largely adopted in the Trg. this sign of the R. is dropped as being no more very necessary"³. He adds further⁴ "In the more composite developement of this system, D. is not only indicated by the form of the preceding vowel-sign but also by the point within the letter. This is really not necessary, and can only be explained by the adoption into the Spl. system of a feature belonging to the Sbl. punctuation". Of our MSS. A and B unfortunately show a slight corruption in fitfully employing the D. point and C regularly uses the R. sign as Margoliouth has remarked. But D has neither the one nor the other. Many instances of the D. are to be found in A. This MS. although apparently using the Sbl. vocalization transcribes the Spl. into the Sbl. This may account for the frequency of the D. point in this MS. Here are a few exemples דִקְלַיָּא 1, 7, חֲזֵה 1, 24, דְּאִתְיְהִב 1, 26, דָּךְ 1, 26, דַּהֲוָה 2, 11, דָּכֵּה 2, 16, דָּהּ 2, 18, דְּיִשְׁרֵא 2, 19, דִּקְלָא 2, 23.

¹ Cf. VI, 8.   ² Cf. Dalman l. c. p. 46.   ³ l. c. p. 46.
⁴ l. c. p. 49.

By the existence of so many examples in two chapters it might perhaps be thought that the sign was very frequently employed throughout the MS.; but the scribe breaks off suddenly and we find whole series of chapters which do not contain a solitary D.

The following are a few examples from *B*. הֲוָ֔ה 1, 11, בְּרֵאשִׁ֔ית 1, 11, הֲוָ֔ה 1, 28, כָּ֔ל 1, 29, הֲוָ֔ה 1, 31. *A* has none of these!

In the specimen chapter appended to this investigation I have followed *D* which is the most perfect MS. and has neither D. nor R. sign.

8) The absence of all these signs, shows that the Aramaic of the Yemen MSS. is much more closely akin to the Bb. Aram. and Syriac than is the case with our European editions of the Trg., and it may be seen how appropriate the Spl. vocalization is to the Aramaic language.

9) Our MSS. agree with Bb. Aram. in many grammatical points.

a. 3rd. Pers. Sin. Fem. Suffix ends in הַ—. Cf. Daniel 2, 11 רַגְלַהּ.

b. 1st Pers. Sin. and Pl. Suffixa of Verb are resp. ־ַנִי and ־ַנָא with P. Cf. Dan. 2, 9 הַחֲוֹדְעֻנַּנִי.

c. 3rd. Pers. Plu. Fem. Perf. of Verb ends in ה. Cf. Dan. 5, 5 נְפַקָה[1].

d. 2nd. Pers. Sin. Suffix is punctuated with Q. Cf. Dan. 4, 22 מָרְלָךְ.

e. Our MSS. punctuate many words with P. corresponding to the Bb. Aram. form with S. whilst B. punctuates with H. e. g. בְּרָהּ חֲדָא שְׂעָרֵהּ הֶלְבָּא.

f. Miscellaneous words such as מֶבְדְּהוֹן וְגַפֵּי צִפְּרַיָּא שַׂבְיָא agree in the two dialects.

---

[1] Or. 2374 writes thus, although Merx's edition of Daniel [Leipzig, 1882] has the Ketib נְפַק but Q'ré נְפַקָה.

VI. VOCALIZATION.

1. Before considering the changes which the pronunciation underwent on being transferred from the Spl. to the Sbl. punctuation, it may be remarked that the Yemen MSS. do not show that superfluity of vowel-letters which is found in our Targum editions[1]. As B. remarks "this redundancy of vowel-letters points back to a time when no vowels were yet written and when the vowel-signs were subsequently added these letters should have been struck out, their retention giving rise to much confusion"[2]. As instances we may notice such words as זֵד and שָׁבְלֵי which B. writes זַאֲרִי and עַרְבְלַאֲ where the א merely points out the ā sound.

2. In considering the differences shown by the MSS. and the European-Babylonian texts it will be seen by tracing words to their etymologies that the former present a more accurate pronunciation. Now as it is extremely improbable that the scribes were acquainted with the etymologies of the words which they wrote, this shows that they must have been conscientious in preserving the correct original orthography.

3. B.'s edition of the Trg. has many words punctuated with P. which appear in the MSS. with Q. a. Monosyllabic words and Particles: בֹּר (Syriac ܒܪ) 2, 9. לֵיה (Syriac ܠܗ) 2, 19. קֵל (Syriac ܩܠ) 3, 8.—b. 3rd Person Singular Preterite Peal of the Verbs יִש. הֵי 2, 3, בֵּחֵי 6, 6. This corresponds to the Syriac Form.—c. On the other hand, the MSS. differ from the Syriac in the 3rd Person Singular Preterite Peal of the Verba Mediae Geminatae[3] e. g. בֵּז 16, 4. Syriac would here punctuate the ז with Petaḥa. But cf. דָּק Dan. 2, 35.—d. In the case of the Present Participle the MSS.

---

[1] Likewise in Christian Palestinian Aramaic the matres lectionis are less used. (Cf. Nöldeke l. c. p. 447.)   [2]) Berliner l. c. p. 133.
[3] For the contrary process we may compare the Hebrew זַ Zechar. 4, 10 (Pret. of בז) as if it were from בז and שָׁת (for שָׁת) Isaiah 44, 18.

again show agreement with the corresponding Syriac form. e. g. הֵיתִיבִ 4, 20, הֲדִרִי 4, 21, הַשְׁלֵט 17, 16.—e. The Q. of the 3rd Person Singular Feminine of the Preterite of Verba ל"א is difficult to explain[1]. Cf. הֲוָת 3, 20 קָמַת 4, 25.— f. The Spl. System is undoubtedly more correct in punctuating the Suffix of the 2nd Pers. Sin. with Q. Cf. בֵּיתָךְ 45, 9, מַלְכּוּתָךְ 17, 5, לָךְ 19, 15. So also B. Aram. cf. עֲלָךְ Dan. 6, 13. —g. Miscellaneous words, the majority of which agree with the corresponding Syriac forms. אֱדַיִן 1, 11 (Syriac ܗܝܕܝܢ), בָּנָת 8, 9 (Syriac ܒܢܬ). On the other hand B. has the Q. in many instances in which the MSS. write P.: a. Suffix of the 3rd Person Singular Feminine הֵילָהּ 4, 12. This agrees with the B. Aram. form. Cf. בַּהּ Daniel 4, 14, חֲמָתֵהּ Dan. 2, 11[2].—b. The vowel of the 2nd radical of a verb is frequently P. just as in the corresponding words in Syriac הַהֵימִיב 1, 29, יְדִיעוּ 3, 7.—c. Since, as will be seen more clearly below, the pause has little influence in the Spl. punctuation herein showing the small influence of the Massorah of the Hebrew text, our MSS. retain the P. in many cases where B. has a pausal Q. חַי 1, 5, מַלְכּוּתָהּ 1, 22.— d. The vowel before the suffixes נָא and הּ is P. in the MSS. בְּבָבֶלְנָא 1, 26, הֲקִימֵהּ[3] 4, 14.—e. The absence of Še. Compositum may account for such instances as בָּרַת 3, 13, אֲחַוְיָא 13, 8.

4. We have now arrived at the second pair of kindred vowels Ḥ. and Ṣ. Only a couple of instances are here given of words which are written by B. with Ṣ. but are found in the MSS. with Ḥ. and vice versa, but it may be

---

[1] But Biblical Aramaic likewise עֲנָת Dan. 7, 19 and אֲמֶרֶת ib. 7, 22.
[2] Philippi tells us that the original form was probably Qameṣ in Biblical Aramaic, "Scribitur autem ־ָה pro ־ַהּ quia, ut Masora Targumo Onkelosiani ostendit, sermo posterior ā et a uti pronuntiatione sic etiam scriptione commiscere consuevit. Vocalem huius terminationis origine longum esse ex אָה־ apparet, quod targumice in locum antiquioris ah successit". (v. Libri Danielis, Ezrae et Nehemiae ed. Baer, l. c. p. LVIII.) [3] So also in B. Aram. Cf. הֲקִימֵהּ Daniel 7, 16.

added that in the majority of examples which I have noted the reading of the MSS. may be verified by reference to the etymologies of the words or to their corresponding Syriac forms. B. has Ṣ. with such words as אָרִיתִ֗ 2, 19, הָקִ֗ים 13, 2. But Ḥ. with גִּבּוֹרִ֗ 3, 22, קָיְמָא֗ 8, 22.

5. The 3rd pair of kindred vowels are Ḥo. and Š. These interchanges appear to depend greatly upon the pronunciation of these sounds. Thus B. writes the words שׁוּם 3, 20, פּוּם 4, 21 with Šureq; and the latter punctuation seems, at first sight, more correct, but, it must be borne in mind that Š. and Ḥo. are represented by one sign only in Jacobite Syriac. The Nestorians pronounced ܝܡܽܘܿܢ as if it were written with a Ḥolem[1]; whilst, on the other hand, they pronounced ܝܡܽܘܢ as the ordinary u sound[2]. Perhaps the Yemenite Jews pronounced the words פּוּם and שׁוּם—which are written with ܦܽܘܡ in Jacobite Syriac—as pōm and šōm, but having a distinct vowel-sign for Ḥo., they punctuated it with Ḥo. For B. Ḥo. and MSS. Š. v. Part II.

6. Before noticing the other numerous interchanges among vowels in the two systems, it must be noticed that the vowel of the Imperfect seems to vary between F. and P. in the MSS. May we not trace the P. to Arabic influence? In that language the vowel of the Servile Prefix is Fatḥa. We might naturally expect that MSS. hailing from Yemen in South Arabia would present some Arabic characteristics and that this is the case may be seen by the following examples 14, 23 אֶכֶּב (C אֵכֶּב), 15, 8 אַדַע but C אֵדַע. In these instances,

---

[1] Cf. Duval, Grammaire Syriaque, Paris 1881, pp. 47—48. [2] So also Nöldeke in his article on Christian Palestinian Aramaic l. c. p. 456 "The ܘܿ (ōn) in ܬܓܚܟܘܢ "you laugh" disagrees with the pronunciation in East Syriac. We should expect ܘ (un)". Dalman l. c. p. 63) remarks "The superlinear vocalization of the Targums, and usually also the Tiberian, has in the form of the Masculine a long ō as in פֹּם שֹׁם which however becomes u in the derived forms. The Tiberian vocalization clearly stands here in closer relation with the old Palestinian usage".

we see that C inclines more to the forms which we find in our Trg. editions, a fact which may be often noticed in the instances which will be quoted later on.

7. Variations in punctuation:

a) B.H.=MSS. P. הִתְכַּנַּשׁ¹ 1, 27, אֻחְדָּה 6, 20.

b) B.P.=MSS. H.; יִתְחֲזֵי 4, 20 (but C יִתְחֲזֵא), יִתְבְּנֵא 9, 5 (but C and D יִתְבְּנֵה). I . justifiable in both instances².

c) B.Ṣ.=MSS. P. יֵאתֵא 4, 3, מִשְׁתַּלְחִין 14, 18.

d) B.P.=MSS. Ṣ. אָפֵס 15, 10.

e) B.P.=MSS. Ho. שְׁלִיט 3, 16, הִרְבִּית 16, 4. Both these are given by Levy.

f) B.Ho.=MSS. Ṣ. קְיָם (A קִיָּם) 4, 6. Here again the Ṣ. is more correct since קְיָם is a Noun; Levy also קְיָם.

g) On the other hand, the MSS. have Ho. where B. reads Ṣ. in פְּרִיסַת 2, 24 which is as incorrect as B.'s פְּרִיסָה the correct form being פְּרִיסָא.

h) A has the modified ü sound³ which is certainly a vulgarism and which, according to Wright, was heard dialectically in Old Arabic and is found occasionally in the vulgar dialects⁴. For instance, in the word מַלְכּוּת=מַלְכֻּת 19, 34⁵.

i) B. כְּתִיבָא where the MSS. give כְּתִיב 4, 21.

j) MSS. אָחֳרָן. B. אָחֳרִין 4, 25.

k) MSS. מְבַהֲלָה (C and D more correctly the Pael מְבַהֲלָא). B. מְבַהֲלָן.

l) Finally, the Yemen MSS. punctuate with Šureq

---

¹ Cf. כַּפָּתוּ Dan. 3, 15. ² v. Levy, Chaldäisches Wörterbuch, s. v. Leipzig 1866. ³ Strangely enough the reverse process is mentioned by Nöldeke as taking place in Christian Palestinian Aramaic. "We find u where we should expect i as in ܟܣܦܐ (Hebrew כֶּסֶף)" p. 456. Dalman mentions that Franz Delitzsch asserted that in the time of the Punctatores in Palestine u was pronounced ü (Dalman, l. c. p. 63). ⁴ Wright, "Comparative Grammar of the Semitic Languages", Cambridge 1890, p. 77. ⁵ Cf. also the writing of the Arabic sound Plural Nominative in īna for ūna which is common in the Yemenite Jewish-Arabic texts. v. also Duval , l. c. p. 47.

where B. has P.[1] in בְּרִיָּת 1, 10, גְּבִיאַ 4, 1. In the latter instance Bevan says the change is due to the following labial[2]; בְּטוּלִם 4, 12, בִּיאַ 14, 17, בִּיאַ 41, 40. For the two last examples Levy prefers Pataḥ. It can be seen at a glance that the MSS. readings are superior.

8. The Še.Mobile is much more frequently employed in the Spl. system than is the case in the Sbl., since it is also used with the Gutturals, in which case the Sbl. system replaces it by Še.Compositum. It must now be noticed that interchanges between Še. and the full vowels are frequently met with: a) B. P.: MSS. Še. אֲזַל 3, 8, לְמִפַּל 11, 6. The first instance is Etpeel whilst B. reads, perhaps more correctly Etpaal; this will be fully considered when treating of the conjugations. The word לְמִפַּל being Afel of נְפַל has Še. correctly. — b) B. Q.: MSS. Še. אֲזַל 3, 17, נְפַל 5, 1. These being Preterites of Verba, have Še. just as we find in Syriac. — c) B. Ṣ.: MSS. Še.; אֲזַל 3, 15, אֲזַלְנָא 3, 20. For the latter cf. B. Aram. אֲזַל Dan. 2, 10. The Sbl. vocalization as exhibited in B.'s edition of the Trg., clearly shows the influence of the Hebrew language in these examples. — d) B. Še.: MSS. Ṣ. בַּס 5, 1. Levy, s. v. allows either form in this instance. — e) B. Ḥ.: MSS. Še. בְּחֶדְוָה 2, 2, חֲדִי 4, 1.

9. That the Yemenite Jews were most careful in preserving the correct traditional pronunciation of the Trg. is shown most clearly by Derenbourg in his "Manuel du Lecteur". "They have still preserved the old-fashioned and good custom of translating each verse in public; a little boy nine or ten years of age stands on the platform and recites the Targum of each verse after the Reader has cited the Hebrew". "Further", says M. Derenbourg, „they have preserved a more exact tradition of the Targum, whereas we know of other countries where the Chaldean Version was already neglected in the 11th century"[3].

[1] Cf. Chr. Pal. Aram. "u sometimes stands for a as in ܐܘܢ ܠܗܘܢ (אֲזַלְנָא) p. 455. [2] Book of Daniel. Cambridge 1892, p. 81. [3] l. c. p. 509.

The use of Še.Mobile for the semi-vowels shows that this Še. must have had a much more distinct pronunciation than we are accustomed to give it, and it is a fact that oriental Jews sound the Šewa just as the occidental Jews pronounce Segol even at the present day[1].

When the Še.Compositum is represented in the MSS. by Še.Quiescens we may assume that the pronunciation was a more hurried one, whilst the full vowel would indicate a longer or fuller pronunciation. In connection with the pronunciation of Hebrew in use among the Jews of Yemen it is instructive to notice Derenbourg's description of the account given by Jacob Sappir[2] of the present pronunciation of Hebrew by the Yemenite Jews. "As regards their vowels they pronounce Q. and P. like the Germans, contracting the lips for the former and opening the mouth wide for the latter, the Ḥo. they pronounce as the Polish Jews, the Ṣ. like the Spaniards and the S. like a very short P., so as to distinguish it from its original P. The Še.Mobile is pronounced in different ways; before a guttural it takes the vowel which that letter has, before a Yod it has that of Ḥ., everywhere else it resembles a weak *a*. There are also people at Yemen who speak less correctly, who confound S. and P. and pronounce Še.Mobile with a full vowel and ignorant or neglectful scribes make these errors current in their copies of the Pentateuch or the Prayers"[3].

In the segoleted forms we know the 2nd P. is only a help-vowel and it was probably pronounced as we pronounce the S.[4] That P. was sometimes read as an *ĕ* sound may

---

[1] Cf. The Codd. Gaster No. 146,a 14th century Karaite MS. from Nisibis; Nos. 155, 159, 160 Maḥazor Byzant. Rite (XVII and XVIII cent.) and Codd. Montefiore 444, 445 and 446 Maḥazor Corfu. which write Še. where we would expect S. and vice versa; employing Ṣ., S. and Še. indiscriminately. Thus we read עֲצֵי־ , בְּרֵכַת בִּכְלִי־עֲצֵי and עֲצֵי immediately followed by אֲצֵי.   [2] In his אבן ספיר (Lyck 1866).   [3] Manuel du Lecteur, l. c., pp. 510—511.   [4] So also in Christian Palestinian Aramaic in such words as ܫܢܬܐ (ܫܢܬܐ) "Year" ܥܡ (ܥܡ) "with" (Nöldeke l. c. p. 454).

perhaps be seen from Proverbs 12, 28 where the Septuagint, Pešitta and Targum all render אַל־מָוֶת as if it were written אֶל־מָוֶת. Cf. also Jeremiah 13, 21 יֹאחֲזוּךְ where we should expect יֹאחֲזוּךְ. Dr. Gaster has pointed out that Prayer-Books from Corfu give to the Še. the full vowel-sign ĕ or ē almost invariably[1]. He also points out that the pronunciation of Še. usually heard at the present day is undoubtedly incorrect, according to the opinion of all the old grammarians from the Dikduke ha-te'amim till Kimḥi. The ancient LXX transcriptions of שְׁלֹמֹה and עֲמוֹרָה as Solomon and Gomorrah point to a similar conclusion[2]. Cf. also the remarks of Margoliouth on the Spl. vocalization[3]. b) In connection with the pronunciation it may be noticed that the Yemen scribes made no alteration in the vocalization to indicate the Pause. This pausal influence is a characteristic of the Hebrew and not of the Aramaic language. The rarity of any vocalic alteration under the pausal influence in Bb. Aram. is a sufficient proof of this fact. Even in Bb. Aram. many examples are to be found where H. is employed where no pause occurs and where we might consequently expect S. Cf. כֹּל Daniel 6, 21, מִצַּלְּלֵהּ Dan. 7, 8, בְּצַל Ezra 4, 23, שָׂם Ezra 6, 12, בְּצַע Dan. 4, 11. We may compare its use in our MSS. to that of the Aramaic portions of the Bible[4]. We there notice only a few instances with Silluq and Sof Pasuq where P. is changed into Q. and S. becomes H. Berliner says in his Massorah[5]:—"Both schools (*i. e.* the Babylonian and Palestinian) have the use of the Pause with Athnach and Sof-Pasuq, whilst with the Sureans the Pause is also used with Sakef. In the case of Genesis 18, 30 there seems no difference between the two schools, both schools reading a pausal form at this Sakef". The word Berliner refers to in this passage is אֲצַלְּלֵהּ and yet all the

---

[1] M. Gaster "Die Unterschiedlosigkeit zwischen Pathaḥ und Segol" in Stade's Zeitschrift, Giessen 1894, p. 62.   [2] p. 61.   [3] l. c. p. 47.
[4] v. Kautzsch, "Grammatik des Biblisch-Aramäischen", Leipzig 1884, p. 39.   [5] Leipzig 1877, Introduction, p. XX.

four MSS. read here אִכֵּלָל. Similarly our MSS. read כֹּל 24, 33, הֵיכָל 44, 2. So כַּפִּי 21, 7. But here and there we notice the Athnaḥ causing a change of vowel e. g. הֵא 4, 2. C lengthens more frequently e. g. הַיְכִין 12, 5, נָאָיִ 8, 7, at a Sakef; the other MSS. having S. A has נַעֵּי at an Athnaḥ, the remaining MSS. again showing a S. Berliner in his Massorah says the form כְּתֵב is only used in Pause when punctuated with Ḥ., but our MSS. read כְּתֵב in 24, 1, 27, 1 and 35, 29, where there is no pause. On the other hand they have אֱלֹהֵי 36, 11 at Athnaḥ where B. has a P. We also notice the influence of the Pause in לְיָרֵהּ 38, 13, אֱלֹהִים 41, 52 (but A אֱלָהִין) and הֵיכָל 46, 6. Yet the cases where we find a pausal influence in our MSS. are extremely rare, and hence we see that the influence of the Hebrew original upon the text of the Trg. punctuated according to the Spl. vocalization is comparatively insignificant. It may be noted that most of the examples I have quoted are Proper Names which were probably punctuated in these cases exactly as they occur in the Hebrew text.

10. From all these examples it may be seen what great differences are noticeable in the two systems. In general, the Spl. system approaches the Bb. Aram. and Syriac forms, which we should naturally expect in an Aramaic language, whilst the Sbl. system shows considerable Hebrew influences. Further, the forms given in the MSS. are etymologically more correct than those found in our editions. In a few instances the surroundings influence the pronunciation.

VII. ORTHOGRAPHY.

1. The orthographical variations shown by the MSS. are numerous and important. I shall here only indicate a few. Lists will be found in Part II and also an attempt to justify the readings of the MSS. a) The following variations may be regarded as due to the influence exercised by dialect.

B. reads אֻמַיָּן 3, 18; the rest have אֻמַיָּא. L. confirms *B*. *A.* בְּגַדְיָא. *B, C, D* בְּחֶסְדָּא 6, 16. *B.* has בְּכַסְיָם. *B.* and *C* אִסְטְלָּוָן 45, 22, *A* and *B* אִסְטְלָא, *D* אִסְטְלָן. L.[1], although noticing the form given by B., gives that of *D* as the best Reading.
—b) The MSS. occasionally make use of vowel-change to distinguish the different meanings of a word. Thus עַל = upon, עָל = he went up; בַּר = son, בָּר = besides; אַתְּ = thou, אָת = a sign.—c) *C* has the 3rd Person Plural of Verba ל״א ending in ־ֻ and not in וּ. This peculiarity is pointed out by Berliner in his Massorah (p. 92) as a Syriasm. It is also occasionally found in *B*, but *A* and *D* never show it. As an instance we may take the word אִתְמְלִיאוּ 7, 20. Some variations are also found in Verba ע״י. *A, B* and *D* read בְּמֵיחַדְּ 19, 14, but B. and *C* בְּמֵיחַדְּיִן. Landauer[2] very appropriately refers us here to the Present Participle of the Verba ע״י in Syriac in which language ܩܐܶܡ is pronounced ka-yem. Similarly בְּמֵיחַת would be pronounced as if it were written בְּחַיְּדִין and this latter reading may accordingly be regarded as a popular spelling of בְּמֵיחַדְּיִן[3].—d) We sometimes find interchanges of letters consistently occurring; thus ס is used by the MSS. in cases where B. writes שׂ. The latter is not an Aramaic letter at all, but is imported from the Hebrew. *A* has it incorrectly in two places where a שׂ is to be read viz. קְסַם 9, 13 and בְּסַמָא 19, 17.—ש and ס. *B* and *D* have יָהֵב 31, 42. The Rest יְהִיב. All have פֵּן 31, 27. B. פֵּשׁ which the author of the Pathṣegen[4] has already pointed out as standing for the more usual פֵּן, as Landauer remarks s. v. in his Massorah. All MSS. read הָה where B. and L.[5]

[1] s. v. [2] "Massorah zum Onkelos nach neuen Quellen", Letterbode VII &c. [3] In Biblical Aramaic the Ketib is always with א but the Qeré with ־. Cf. בָּאדַיִן (Qeré בֵּאדַיִן) Daniel 2, 38; 3, 31; 6, 26, בֵּאדַר (Qeré בֵּאדַיִן) Daniel 4, 23, קָאֲמִין (Qeré קָיְמִין) Daniel 3, 3, דָּאֲרִין Qeré דָּיְרִין) Ezra 7, 25. Cf. also Dalman's Grammar p. 45 "Aus Schreibungen wie מִלְּאיָא für מִלַּיָא, קָאֵם für קָם darf geschlossen werden, dass א zwischen zwei Vokalen als stimmhafte Gaumenspirans gesprochen wurde". [4] Published in Adler's edition of the Targum l. c. [5] s. v.

give אְתָא 16, 12. A and D כָּלְבֵי 40, 18. B. B and C
מלכהּ¹. The ה is a Hebraism, although Bb. Aram. likewise
has it. e) B writes בחרשבניא 14, 1. A, C and D divide the
word בני לשרב and this, at a later time, was looked upon
as the correct traditional writing². The MSS. give יְהוּדָיֵא יְהוּדָיִין
3, 16 and בכשדאי 12, 13 in all of which B. writes יְהוּדָיֵן &c.—
f) The Yemen MSS. do not know of the so-called לשון חוטף
which gives us such forms as קֳדָם and אַחֲוָיָה but write
these words as they are found in the Hebrew Text.— g) By
קרי וכתיב the Massorah meant that several passages should
stand in the Trg. just as they occur in the Hebrew. The
MSS. however appear to ignore this Rule. Thus they all
read אִיתַי (and not אִתָּי) 34, 19, האיתי 27, 46. A and
D read אלהא אמר 27, 2 but here B and C follow the
Hebrew אמר בה. A and C have כתבא on the margin but
כתבה in the Text³ 26, 14. A and D have יתיב but B and
C יתב 23, 6. A, B and D אתה C אתי 39, 1. A and
B read בכתבא כתיבא, C and D כתיבא כתב 15, 18 and
finally B writes the Tetragrammaton instead of אלהים⁴ 9, 6.
By these examples it may be at once seen that the scribes
could not have recognised these rules of קרי וכתיב, or, at
any rate, they were only slightly acquainted with them.—
h) Marginal Readings have already been pointed out occasionally. These glosses are important since they are all added
by a later hand and explain the origin of many words which
afterwards became incorporated with the Text itself. These
marginal readings also constitute an argument for the greater
age and originality of the texts with Superlinear vocalization
which have been preserved to us by the Yemenite Jews.— 3, 23
C has האמרת on the margin, the text of which has been

---

¹ Cf. Ezra 4, 16 where אנחנא stands for the more usual אנחנה so
Or. 2374 has כדי כדנ (Dan. 2, 47) where Baer reads קשט קשוט and
שזיב (Dan. 6, 13) where Baer has שיזב.   ² Cf. Talmud Babli Tr.
Hullin 65a.   ³ The reading כתבא is quoted by Theodorus Mopsuestenus (v. Part II, Ch. II, J).   ⁴ cf. B. l. c. p. 216.

corrected by a later hand to דְּאִתְבְּסִי; but as the word דְאִתְבְּרִי is given by Berliner in his Massorah[1] under thc heading of דָאיִק which means that it is undoubtedly the correct reading, we must reject the correction דְאִתְבְּסִי. 7, 16 C has בְּמֵ־דַּ־יֵּהּ on the margin to be placed between יי and אֱלוֹהִי. We shall see when speaking of the Additions that A and D have this word already inserted in the text. 25, 8 D has רְוּמֵיהּ on the margin to be read after צַלְמָא[1]. B has the same word in its text. 27, 22 C has דְּוִּהָ on the margin but דָּהּ correctly in the text. This has been noticed above under קרא ותרגום. Many more examples of marginal readings will be noticed when we shall treat of the Variant Readings.—i) The Yemen MSS. almost invariably follow the reading given in the Massorah of Berliner under the head of לְנְהַרְדְּעָאֵי which represents a School in Babyl. in favour of the original Plst. Text and is a great argument for the authenticity of the text which is found in these MSS. To give one instance; B. reads גְּזַר and גְּזָרוּ 17, 26 and 27 the MSS. have the Itpeel אִתְגְּזַר and אִתְגְּזָרוּ. Berliner[2] places the Peal reading in the column headed לְסוּרָאֵי whilst the Etpeel is placed under לְנְהַרְדְּעָאֵי. "Perhaps"—adds Berliner—"whether we should take the Peal or Itpeel form depends upon the old grammatical question whether the root of the Hebrew word is גזר or נזר". Baer[3], however, is of a different opinion. He says, speaking of certain forms which occur in B. Aram. and which he treats as Etpeel "Praeteritum huius conjugationis interdum syllabam praeformativam abjicit velut אִתְפְּרֵס = פְּרֵס Daniel 5, 28.

VIII. GRAMMATICAL VARIATIONS.

1. THE NOUN.

a) State. There are a few changes in the different states of the Substantives.

---

[1] l. c. p. 116. [2] Massorah p. 62. [3] Daniel etc. p. LIX.

α) In the Absolute and Emphatic States, which in the MSS. appear to be used almost indiscriminately[1]. Nöldeke informs us that these two states were entirely confused together in the Mandaic dialect of Aramaic[2], and from the examples which will be given in Part II, it will be seen that a similar laxness is noticeable in the Targum as represented in the Yemen MSS. *A, B, D* בֵּאלָהּ 4, 16, B. and *C* אֱלָהָא. The text is בְּאֵרָן; 6, 21, MSS. בֵּירָא, B. בֵּירָה. The corresponding word in the Hebrew Text is בְּאֵרָה.

β) Absolute and Construct. 15, 19—21, in the Patronymics קִינָאָה לִבְנָאָה &c, B. believes we have either a shortened form of the absolute Plural or the Construct State used instead of the Absolute[3]. The first-mentioned explanation is supported by Wright who says final Mim or Nun are apt to fall away in the Absolute Plural of nouns in the Assyrian, Talmudic and Modern Syriac languages[4]. Dalman[5] assumes that these are shortened forms of the Absolute "Statt der

---

[1] The same anomaly is also found in Syriac (cf. Duval's Grammar, Paris 1881, p. 249): "L'état emphatique s'est alors généralisé au point de devenir la forme usuelle, et l'état absolu, que l'on ne rencontre plus que dans quelques tournures de phrase, est souvent difficile à constater".   [2] Mandäische Grammatik, p. 300. Also in the Christian Aramaic dialect of Palestine "We frequently find in the text lying before us the Emphatic State where we should expect the Absolute". He, however, explains these examples as due to later corruption. (Vide ZDMG. XXII, p. 507). Cf. also Berliner l. c. p. 204. But Uhlemann when noticing this apparent confusion in the Samaritan dialect remarks "In haud paucis locis utitur Samaritanus Nomine emph., ubi Hebraeus habet Nomen sine articulo; quae diversitas in eo est querenda, quod Samaritanus forte ibi de re magis definita cogitaret". He gives as example 25, 23 אֵם עִיר עָרֵי of which the Targum is כְּרַךְ שׁוּרַיָּא לִבְרַיָּא and the Samaritan also writes the Emphatic state with both words viz. ᛉᛏᛊᛒ ᛗᛊᚹᛏ ᛉᚱᚱ ("Institutiones Linguae Samaritanae" Uhlemann, Leipzig 1837, p. 196). Even in the Biblical Aramaic Text, the British Museum MS. Or. 2374 disagrees with Baer's Edition in reading פַּר לָא (Daniel 2, 42) where Baer has בְּרַל.   [3] l. c. page 205.   [4] Cf. Wright: l. c. pp. 67, 146 and 147.   [5] l. c. p. 151.

indeterm. Pluralendung īn tritt zuweilen ein die Verkürzung e (ī)". In connection with these Patronymics we may also compare ־ּבִֿ 1, 10 and ־ּבֵּהֿ 14, 1. The MSS. have ־ּרֿ ־ּבֿ 17, 20 whilst B. עֲשַׂר רַּוַּת which, perhaps, corresponds more closely with the Hebrew original שְׁנֵים־עָשָׂר and which is also given by L. s. v.; 40, 16 B ־ּבֿ which is probably a Hebraism. B., A, C, D, correctly, רַּבִֿ.

b) Number. Turning from the consideration of the differences in States to those observable in Number, it is at once noticeable that these variations are both more numerous and more important. The differences may very frequently be explained as due to the Targumist's desire to give rather the sense of the Hebrew than a mere slavish rendering; whilst some are due to an uncertainty whether a Collective Noun should be treated as Singular or as Plural. B. and A ־ּהֿ 4, 11. B and C הּ־ּהֿ, D הּבָא. The first reading appears to be the best, and is given by L.[1], since we expect here the Plural Construct. B and C may be true to the Aramaic idiom; but D appears, at first sight, to be incorrect. Nevertheless this reading cannot be condemned, since the sense of the passage is certainly singular. B. רַאשֵׁי MSS. רֵאשַׁיְ 1, 21. The Subject is עָם, which, being a Collective Noun may possibly justify either reading. L., however, gives the same as that of the MSS. C ־ּהֿ B., A, B and D ־ּהֿ 14, 22. Luzz. in his 'Philoxenos'[2] asserts that the Plural is necessary here, since the Targumist refers the passage to Prayer in which both hands are held up, whilst the Hebrew text refers to an oath, for which only one hand is raised.

c) The peculiar use of the Genders in the MSS., and the apparent confusion which exists in the use of Masculine for Feminine presents us with a grammatical problem. Did the primitive Aramaic language have distinct forms for the Masculine and Feminine Genders or was this distinction merely the result of a later development and differentiation

---

[1] s. v.   [2] Vienna: 1830, p. 35.

fixed by the Massorites and Grammarians? The written text of the Aramaic of the Bible seems to point to one form for the two Genders; when, however, the suffix refers to a feminine object it was differently punctuated by the Massorites. Bevan, referring to this phenomenon in Bb. Aram. remarks that the written text is grammatically inaccurate: "Sometimes grammatical inaccuracies which probably were found already in the primitive text have been corrected by the later vocalizers; thus הן the suffix of the 3rd Person Plural was used indifferently for the Masculine or Feminine, but has been marked with the vowel ē whenever it refers to a feminine Noun. Similarly in the 3rd Person Plural of the Perfect of the Verb the termination ו is used for both genders, but has been treated as ā by the vocalizers, when the Subject is Feminine"[1]. So also the Yemen MSS. use the termination הן and כן both for Masculine and Feminine and likewise the suffix ון is used as Common Suffix of the 3rd Person Plural of the Imperfect of Verbs where we should expect Mas. ון and Fem. ן—[2]. I have only noticed a few exceptions to this rule in C and shall later on enumerate these. In my opinion these examples are not due—as Bevan thinks—to grammatical inaccuracies but are really of Common Gender[3]. We may perhaps find analogous instances in the

---

[1] Bevan: l. c. p. 39.   [2] Although the regular fem. forms were mostly used in Christian Palestinian Aramaic still we find examples in which the Masc. endings are used for the Fem. as in اجبـﻪ (ZDMG. XXII. p. 474).   [3] The text of Daniel in the British Museum MS. Or. 2374; appears to confirm this assumption. As I have already remarked this MS. pays no attention to the כתיב but inserts the קרי in its text. In this MS. then the scribe writes בניה Dan. 2, 33 when our editions of the Bible say we must read בניך on account of the Gender, although the כתיב is בניה. Now had the scribe read בניך he would have undoubtedly written the word thus. This proves that in the time and place of the scribe this word was pronounced בניה just as it is written and that the reading בניך was unknown to the scribe.

Hebrew language in which the word נַעַר[1] originally meant both 'boy' and 'girl' being spelt without ה when it occurs in the Pentateuch. But a much more striking instance of the same phenomenon is to be found in the Hebrew הוא which in the Pentateuch is the Ketib both for הוא and הִיא (the latter form occurring but 11 times in the whole Pentateuch, according to the Massorites)[2]. Whether then this peculiarity of the Yemen MSS. is a vulgarism or a classical characteristic of the language remains doubtful, but after observing that a similar phenomenon existed in the primitive Hebrew language, there is no reason why we should not assume that it is likewise characteristic of the primitive Aramaic language. I now enumerate the few exceptions which I have noticed in C. This MS. reads אֲבוּהוֹן 19; 33, 35 and 38 שֻׁמְשֵׁיהֹן 27, 29 אֲבֻלֵיהוֹן 31, 5 (although in the very same verse we find C giving לְהוֹן and referring the Suffix to the same feminine Subject!) and יָקְמִין[3] 41, 30.

---

[1] Gesenius points out this peculiarity: "The Pentateuch certainly contains some peculiarities of language which have the appearance of archaisms. When these books were composed the words הוא 'he' and נַעַר "young man" were still of common Gender and used also for 'she' and 'young woman'. Vide Gesenius, Hebrew Grammar, Translated by Conant. London 1839. §§ 2. 3.   [2] We find an apparent inconsistency in Ezekiel 23, 45 where אִישׁים refers to a Feminine Subject. In Verse 47 the word is written אִישִׁים.   3 Samaritan (as A, B and D) יקימין. In the following pages some readings from the Samaritan Targum which agree with one or another of the Variant Readings under consideration have been inserted. Since Samaritan has no vowel signs these instances are only of value in confirming the Consonantal Text. Upon the much-vexed question whether the Samaritan Targumist was influenced by the Targum of Onkelos or agreement between the two is due to later interpolations into the Text of the Samaritan Targum I refrain to enter; but bearing in mind that the language of Onkelos and Samaritan are two kindred dialects of Aramaic and that they both represent very ancient Translations of the Hebrew Text, the examples given may be of some value in helping to confirm a reading. The edition of Dr. Adolf Brüll (Frankfort: 1879) has been, in all cases, the text of the Samaritan Targum referred to.

These are evidently mere anomalies, and of no importance. It is unnecessary to give examples here as they occur throughout all the MSS. invariably. Other variations in Gender will be found in Part II.

2. THE VERB.

a) The Conjugations. Very numerous interchanges are to be observed in the Conjugations.

α) Peal and Pael. B הֲסִים. B. A, C, D סַּמֵּי¹ 31, 54. Landauer² explains and justifies the latter reading in his Massorah. He says that here only נְסִיכָא סַּמַּם is mentioned, and hence the Peal is the correct Conjugation. The case is different in Numbers 22, 40 in which example the Pael is necessary, since Balaq offered up a large number of animals (רַב זָבַח). A, B and D הֲשַׁלְאָתָהּ³. B. and C וּשַׁלְאָתָהּ 37, 15. L. gives no Pael of this root, but it may be observed that in the Syriac language the Pael has the same signification as the Peal.

β) Peal and Afel. B. and C אָמַר, A, B, D אֵימַר 4, 3. Similarly throughout Genesis. Now, there is no doubt that A, B and D have the only correct reading of the Afel of אמר cf. Syriac ܐܡܪ. B.'s form is really 1st Per. Sin. Imperf. Peal. B. וְאֶשְׁכְּחִין MSS. have וְהַשְׁכַּחִין 4, 14. The Afel, is the more convenient form, according to L.; this form being preferred to avoid the confusion which might arise in the employment of the Aramaic root שׁכח = to find and the Hebrew root שׁכח = to forget.

γ) Peal and Etpaal, Etpeel or Ettafal. MSS. הִתְרְמִיב (Peal) B. הִתַּרְמַב (Ettafal) 3, 19. The Hebrew שָׁכוּב being an Infinitive may be either Active or Passive. Here it seems to bear an active signification, which would confirm the reading of the MSS. L.⁴ also gives the Peal form here, but Pathšegen⁵ supports B.'s reading and explains it reflectively.

---

¹ Samaritan סַמַּם.   ² Massorah s. v.   ³ Samaritan אֲשַׁלְאָתָהּ.
⁴ s. v.   ⁵ To this verse.

C

B, C and B. וֹסְלִק֨ [1] *A* and *D* יָאסֹלִק (Etpaal) 26, 23. The Hebrew text being יִיעַל appears to confirm the first-mentioned reading. *A* and *D* דְּיִלִידָה [2] B. *B* and *C* דְּאִיתְיְלִיד (Etpeel) 46, 22. The Hebrew is יֻלָּד. The first-mentioned reading, although giving the sense of the original, is less literal than the passive construction.

δ) Pael and Afel. B. אֲיַחַר MSS. אַיְחַר 34, 19. Both these forms have the same meaning, but Berliner, in his Massorah [3], places the reading אִיחַר among the list of instances included under the head of קרא ותרגום and we have already seen that the MSS. appear to take no notice of this Massoretic rule. L. gives אֲיַחַר as Pael of אחר, but as the Pael of אחר occurs very rarely whilst the Afel is fairly common, the reading of the MSS. appears to be preferable. B. וְשַׂדְיָת MSS. וְאַשְׁדִּיאַת 38, 14. In Berliner's Massorah [4] we read לסוראי שדיאת לנהרדעאי אשדיאת to which the author of the Pathsegen adds "There is some difficulty in understanding what difference the Suraans make between ושדיאת when used as the Trg. of ותסר and when it is the Trg. of ותהר as in 4, 1". This implies that he preferred or expected the reading ואשדיאת. L. [5] also prefers the Afel which means to 'depart', 'go away', 'take off', whilst the Pael means 'to conceive'. [6]

ε) Etpeel and Etpaal. MSS. וְאִשְׁתַּדִּית, B. וְאִשְׁתַּדִית 3, 10. Merx in his "Chrestomathia Targumica" [7] pleads for the Etpeel reading "Editiones Itpaal saepe praebent, at observa syr. Etpe. esse abscondit se, absconditus est; Etpa. vero inhumatus est. Payne-Smith s. v." Similarly in 4, 14. *A, B, D* יִתְאֲמַר, B. and *C* יִתְאֲמַר 42, 19. L. [8] here gives the Etpaal, but according to Brockelmann's Lexicon Syriacum [9] the Etpeel is the conjugation in use in the Syriac language. By the examples given in Part II it will be found that this is very frequently the case.

---

[1] Samaritan וסלק.   [2] Samaritan דילדת.   [3] p. 58.   [4] p. 63.
[5] s. v.   [6] But Dalman l. c. p. 39 gives the meaning of both Pael and Afel "schwanger werden".   [7] p. 207.   [8] s. v.
[9] Berlin 1895, p. 21 a.

b) The Tenses.

α) Perfect and Imperfect. 31, 27; B., C and D יֵשׁתַּחֲוִן, A and B הִשְׁתַּחֲוִין but Berliner[1], Landauer[2] and Adler[3] all support the former reading. C הֲוֵי, B., A, B and D הֲוָה 49, 22. The latter reading is correct.

β) Perfect and (Participle) Present. More numerous variations are here noticeable. These differences are mainly due—says B.[4]—to the fact that the Hebrew language has no Present Tense, whilst the Aramaic has no Imperfect with ו conversivum. A, B and D יָפֵק, B. and C יָפֵיק. The Hebrew is יֵצֵא 8, 7. L.[5] supports the former reading which may be taken as correct. MSS. הִתְאָחֵי, B. הִתְחַבְּרִי. The Hebrew is חֶבְרוּ 23, 11. The Hebrew is thus Perfect in form but Present in signification; hence, B.'s reading gives the correct sense but the MSS. have a more literal rendering.

γ) Imperfect and (Participle) Present. B יָפֵק, C יָפֵק, D יָפֵק, A and B. יָפֵק 24, 13. Pathšegen[6] reads as B but it may be observed that D corresponds exactly to the Hebrew תוֹצִיא. B יַפְלִה 43, 25, B., A, C and D אַפְלֵא the latter receiving the support of Pathšegen[7]. B is a literal translation of the Hebrew יַפְלִיא.

c) Other Differences. There are one or two other slight variations to be noticed with the Verb. A and D יִוָּרֵד[8] (Passive), B., B and C יוֹרִיד (Active) 34, 22. The Hebrew being בַּלֶּחֶם; the passive construction is superior. B., A and C הַגִּישׁ, B and D הוּגַּשׁ[9] 13, 16. The latter is the literal translation of the Hebrew הִגִּישׁ. Similarly in 31, 1, B., C and D have הֵאִירוּ whilst A and B read לְהָאִיר this being a translation of the Hebrew לְהָאִיר.

IX. OTHER VARIATIONS.

1) We find a large number of additions, mostly of small words or prepositions in our MSS. Many of these additions

---

[1] Massoráh, p. 98. [2] Massorah s. v. [3] יַעֲלוּ הָרָה to this verse. [4] l. c. p. 203. [5] s. v. [6] To this verse. [7] Samaritan has יַפְלִיא [8] Samaritan likewise יוֹרִיד. [9] Samaritan הוּגַּשׁ.

make the text clearer; others have Halachic reasons, whilst a few are mistakes. We likewise find omissions, that is to say there are less words given in the MSS. than are to be found in B.'s Edition. Some are omitted to save the scribe the trouble of rewriting a string of Proper Names: the verse, as Berliner points out, being read thrice in Hebrew, instead of being followed by its Targum and then by its Arabic translation. Occasionally these omissions are due to the scribe's carelessness.

2) Additions. All the MSS. insert היא הֹוָה before רבהון 4, 22. Adler, in his commentary נתינה לגר: regards this as an instance of Homoioteleuton, the preceding verse having היא היה in the text. A adds לְכָמָת after חוֹבָין 4, 23. This may perhaps be a Halachic addition. Vide Adler in נתינה לגר to this verse. 6, 11 A and D simplify this verse by adding בן before קֳדָם.

Some irregularity is observable in the use of ד to express the construct state and a similar laxity occurs in Syriac. Generally, the construction without ד is the more classical one and the use of ד is the more popular construction. This employment of ד being a much freer and looser construction is preferred by the Aramaic language and is much more frequently used than the other construction.

The MSS. add it in דְּבִקְרֵיהּ 2, 11 (Hebrew הַסוֹבֵב) A, B, D דְּשׁוּם[1] C שׁוּם 33, 18. According to Berliner's Massorah[2] the ד is incorrect in verse 18 but necessary in verse 19; since 18 is given as an instance of קרא ותרגום. The little word ית is sometimes added by B and C, mostly, however, incorrectly. C has ית before קליה 21, 17. This ית is copied from the את of the Hebrew text; but inasmuch as the Trg. employs a Passive construction here, ית is evidently incorrect.

ל is added by B in לְכָל[3] 13, 10, a reading which is rejected by the author of the Pathšegen[4]. ו is added by the

---

[1] Samaritan שׁוּם. [2] P. 58. [3] Likewise Samaritan לְכָל.
[4] to this verse.

MSS. in אבבלרא¹ which is against the Hebrew text and in ינברי¹ 33, 13 which follows the original. *A* and *B* add it in בהי 10, 1 not as Hebr. ב is added by *A* and *D* in בלבהין 42, 24 and since the corresponding Hebrew word is בעלבהם this reading is the correct one.

ב is added by *A*, *B* and *C* in בפהר² 42, 21 (B. and *D* בפהר). The reading with ב appears preferable, since it suits the context so admirably.

3. Omissions. I have noticed some scores of omissions, but shall only mention a few which are not due to any oversight on the part of the scribe. Sometimes verses are omitted in their entirety to save space and the scribe's time; this is particularly noticeable in genealogies. For instance 10, 22 and 23, 27—29.

18, 19 *A* omits הרבן which does not correspond to any word in the Hebrew text but is explained by Adler in his הנה בג בונה "היא בב שדרש ידריל".

18, 30 *B* omits בבלרא which again has no equivalent in the Hebrew text.

19, 7 *C* omits בנן and Pathšegen also remarks that there is no occasion for this word in the Targum text since בנש = אנ.

43, 15 *A* and *D* omit ירהי¹ which is again represented by no word in the Hebrew text, but Raši explains the word as necessary, since, in Aramaic, different Verbs are in use to indicate the seizure of things and the seizure of human beings. נסב being used of things and דבר of men. B. inserts a ד before the following words which I write as they appear in the MSS. הפךר 3, 9; יאהן 7, 22; בלבא 18, 6; אראמהר³ 19, 16; בכל³ 23, 19 (*A* and *D* only); בלבן 41, 39.

An initial י is omitted by *A* and *B* before אמהרר 3, 21. Also before בכל 6, 20 which corresponds to the Hebrew. The

---

¹ Samaritan ינרין. ² Samaritan בפעה. ² Samaritan also ירר and אמרר but, on the other hand, בעל.

MSS. omit הי before פחצי 21, 8. In several other passages the omission of this word is due to the scribe's carelessness.

ל is omitted before למחי 35, 27 by *A*, *B* and *D*; in connection with which we must notice that it does not occur in the Hebrew text. Also before אבוהי 43, 27 where it likewise does not appear in the original, although it does in the following verse. Pathšegen says we must insert the ל in both verses, according to the usage of the Aramaic language. The word הא is omitted by *A* in 48, 22 and by *C* in 32, 18; both passages are however faulty in these MSS.

4) *Contractions*. The scribes regularly contract certain familiar words which constantly recur, especially those in combination with הא and בא.

A has דידך 4, 11. *B*, *C*, *D* דֵה בֹ. *A*, *B* and *D* האנא *C* אנא הא 6, 17 and 9, 9. *A* and *D* בנא. *B* and *C* אך בא 16, 2; 18, 24; 24, 5 &c. *A* and *B* האת, *C* and *D* את הא 20, 3, *C* and *D* במיא, *A* and *B* מן במיא 31, 39. All have בהון 40, 7 and האהון 47, 1.

5) *Interchange of Prepositions and other Particles*. In noting these numerous variations we are again struck with the fact that the manuscript readings are usually superior. MSS. לכל דבחא, B. לכל דבחא 8, 20. B.'s reading is a Hebraism. MSS. ובסומי. B. ובסומיה 49, 9. Berliner in his Massorah[1] places the manuscript reading in the column לבחרדיאי whilst ובסומי is under לסיראי. Besides the examples already quoted of interchanges which take place between different Prepositions, I have to add a number of instances in which different Particles or Prepositions are employed which sometimes completely alter the sense of the passage. I consider it necessary to give these somewhat dry details at length, inasmuch as it is my object to demonstrate the superiority of the Trg. text as exhibited by the MSS. which I have made use of, over the editions which are in current circulation among us at the present day.

[1] p. 63.

B. יָת MSS. יָת 26, 8. The reading יָת is preferable since ית is only used as the sign of the accusative in Aramaic, and not otherwise. Gesenius[1] treats the two Hebrew words את = sign of the accusative, and את = with, as entirely distinct and of different etymology. B., C and D בֵּן, A and B בְּרֵהּ 29, 26, Hebrew is בֵּן. L. reads בֵּן but according to Bernstein-Kirsch's Chrestomathy[2] בֵּן = רִין + בּ and hence either reading may be justified; and this is again the case in 30, 33 where B. reads בֵּן and A, B, D עַל, C is missing. The Hebrew text is בֵּן. The Aramaic verb סָהֵיד may be construed either with בּ or עַל. B. בְּסַכְוָן MSS. בְּסָכְוָן 49, 13. In Berliner's Massorah[3] וּבְסַכְוָן is given as the Suraan and בְּסַכְוָן as the Nehardean reading. L. reads as the MSS. which gives the better sense.

6) We occasionally find variations in the addition of the suffix. B. and C הֲנָאָה, A and D הֲנָאָךְ, B הֲנָאָךְ 4, 7. Berliner, in his Massorah[4], says the suffix is incorrect, but L. reads as the MSS. Likewise, in the variation of the vowel-point L. permits both forms. B. תַקְנָךְ, A, C, D הָנָא, B הָנָא 19, 12. The Hebrew is תִקֵּן. Berliner, in his Massorah,[5] says the Targumist wished to make this word agree in form with the following words בְּיָדֶךָ בְּנַיִךְ both of which have the suffix of the 2nd Person. Pathsegen remarks the same. But this hardly appears to be necessary and the literal translation of the MSS. therefore seems to be superior. B has the word incorrectly punctuated.

X. EXEGETICAL VARIATIONS.

Most of the variations which have been considered hitherto are of importance, showing, as they do, the greater purity of the Aramaic language which the Yemen Trg. Mss. exhibit.

---

[1] Hebrew and Chaldee Lexicon translated by S. P. Tregelles London: 1885 s. v.   [2] s. v. ⇌ (Leipzig 1836).   [3] p. 63.
[4] p. 74.   [5] p. 75.

— 40 —

These Variations give an incentive to the study of these MSS. if for no other reason than their more accurate retention of pure Aramaic forms and expressions.

The exegetical variations, however, are of far greater importance. They cannot be accounted for on the ground of difference of dialect, nor do they point to any linguistic peculiarities, but give a clear reason for assuming that they represent another distinct recension. The chief characteristic of these differences is the preference frequently shown for a literal translation of passages which are in our texts rendered according to traditional Hagadic translations. It has already been pointed out[1] that the preference for literal translations shown by the Plst. recension may perhaps be accounted for by the existence in Palestine of the other Trg. which is certainly of Hagadic character; I refer, of course, to the Targum Jerushalmi; or it may be accounted for as the outcome of a desire to have a translation which should render the Hebrew text in the most faithful and accurate manner, which is also the tendency of Aquilas and all the old translators, who are severely literal. A few instances are given here, the rest will be found in Part II.

26, 22 B. אַרְבִּשְׁיָן, C and D אַרְבִּשְׁרֵי, A and B וְתַרְבֵּי. The Hebrew is וּפְרֵינוּ of which A and B give a literal rendering "God will magnify us and we will multiply ourselves in the land". That this is the valid reading is further proved by the support it receives from Raši and L. The author of the Pathšegen, however, gives a reading similar to that of B. as the correct text "God will magnify and increase us".

30, 15 B., B and D יְדַבֵּרֵי[2], A הַסֵּב, C is missing. Luzz. in his אהב ג[3] points out that those who corrected the original יְדַבֵּרֵי to סֵבָּי made a great mistake, and did not realise the spirit of the Trg. rendering. Onkelos—says Luzz.—undoubtedly wrote יְדַבֵּרֵי but later revisers thought this reading was incorrect since the Infinitive לָקַחַת should require the Infinitive

---

[1] Chap. IV § 4.   [2] Samaritan יִסְחֵי.   [3] p. 25.

ובלהם whilst דתלמין would be the Targum of לקחתם—2nd Feminine Preterite. This, however, Luzz. goes on to say, is not the case; since O. wished to amplify the brevity and clear up the obscurity of the Hebrew passage and accordingly paraphrases דתלמין. Yet in spite of Luzz.'s arguments, one is again inclined to favour the literal translation ובלהם.

30, 22 B reads והוי ־־ ־־ יהי, B., A, C, D והיה לן ־־ למב לחם which is evidently a Hagadic rendering (v. Raši to this verse). B gives the literal translation of the Hebrew text viz ויהי־ אלהים את כל and therefore appears to be the best rendering. 39, 11 B (text) בצמרו בחהרין¹, B (margin), A, C, D and B. בצמק בחהרות. Here we have a good instance of the manner in which marginal glosses crept into the Trg. text. The Hebrew original is לצפעני באסמים of which B is a literal translation. 42, 36. In this verse we see another example of the retention of the original text by B. The Hebrew is אינני which B renders כד־ית־וֹהי whilst B. and the other MSS. give לא הוא לא which gives the sense of the original but is not literal. B.'s translation is also given by L.²

43, 2 B. and C סבקין A, B (margin) and D שיציאו, B (text) erased. Hebrew is כלה. Now the two Aramaic roots סבק and שיצ have the same signification. The authorities differ which word to prefer here. L. remarks that שיצ usually corresponds to the Hebrew כלה³ and Raši likewise reads שיצ. He goes on to say that סבקין is an incorrect reading since the root סבק is only used when one has eaten to satisfaction although some food may still be left, whilst שיציא is used for a man remaining unsatisfied although his supply of food is already exhausted. But Luzz. in his Philoxenos⁴ pleads for the reading סבקין saying that this is the verb employed in Aramaic when the text refers to a 'finishing' with eating, drinking or any other bodily requirement. The

---

¹ Samaritan בחהרות בצמק. ² s. v. ³ Cf. also Ezra 6, 15 שיצי; "And was finished". ⁴ p. 45.

fact that שידאי is given by *B* as a marginal reading seems to support Luzz.'s opinion. It must be noticed, however, that the marginal readings are sometimes preferable and appear to correct a faulty reading which is found in the text. Thus in 45, 11 B., *C, B* (text) read הֹשֵירוּדִי whilst *A*, *B* (margin) and *D* give הֹתמסכן. The Hebrew text is יִמָּךְ. *A*, *B* (margin) and *D* give the best reading since התמסכן = be impoverished whilst הֹשֵירוּדִי has rather the signification of 'be annihilated', 'be undone', 'die'. Raši and Qimḥi both read התמסכן but Pathšegen and Luzz.[1] say we must read הֹשֵירוּדִי for—say they—how can we speak of all one's possessions i. e. one's cattle &c. coming to poverty? But be this as it may the reading התמסכן corresponds exactly with the Hebrew יִמּוּךְ a word which is correctly rendered "come to poverty" in the Revised Version, although it may be noted that some of the Jewish commentators differ in their translation of this word, thus Ibn Ezra "to perish", R. Samuel b. Meir "to be dispossessed", Mendelssohn "to be ruined".

45, 17 *B* (text) אֵרִי[2], *B* (margin), *A, C, D* and B. אובילו. Hebrew באו. The first mentioned reading is preferable since it is quite literal. The reason (says Pathšegen) of the Targumic rendering אובילו is to avoid the redundancy of the Hebrew text and thus render κατὰ σύνεσιν.

46, 1 *B* (text) בסמכא עמא, *B* (margin) and the others הִבְהוֹן חַדָה, Hebrew וָבְהֶם רָעָב. Although *B* (text) is incorrect it is strange that the Trg. of ויבחר זבח in 31, 54 is as he gives here. 47, 20 B. וזבן, MSS. וקנא, Hebrew וַיִּקֶן. B.'s reading וזבן is also quoted by Pathšegen. On the other hand Landauer gives וקנא in his Massorah.[3]

Perhaps B.'s reason is that in this verse Joseph really *bought* the land, whilst in verse 23 he *acquired* the people.

---

[1] אמר נ־. P. 46.   [2] Samaritan יראי.   [3] s. v.

PART II.

CHAPTER I.

Before commencing the lists of examples which illustrate the preceding rules, certain words which call for some comment may here be treated. I believe that most of these words will be found to be more correctly punctuated in the MSS. than in our editions of the Trg. As these words are of constant recurrence their correct vocalization should be fixed. First we have the little word רה. This word, although so exceedingly common is of obscure etymology. Our editions punctuate this word with P. and B. invariably writes רֶה.

L. also writes the word with P., although he compares the syriac ܟܝܳܢ = nature, of which ܟܝܰܢ is construct state. The P. is also supported by Nestle[1], Bernstein-Kirsch and Gesenius in their dictionaries. Merx in his "Bemerkungen über die Vocalisation der Targume"[2] mentions a curious rule which Mercier wished to establish. Mercier wrote רֶה in the Trg. when the corresponding Hebrew is אֶת, but רַה when the text has אֵת. Merx declares most decisively[3] that we are assured that רַה is the correct punctuation by Bar-Ali; רֶה, on the other hand, is invariably incorrect.

Bevan also writes רַה[4], also Duval[5]. Undoubtedly the greatest authority who supports the Q., is the great Orientalist, W. Wright. He remarks:[6] "We get in the first place

---

[1] Syriac Grammar, Berlin: 1889.   [2] Contained in the "Verhandlungen des fünften internationalen Orientalisten-Congresses" Berlin 1881. p. 145.   [3] p. 185.   [4] Bevan: The Book of Daniel p. 38.   [5] Grammaire Syriaque p. 277.   [6] Wright: Comparative Grammar of the Semitic languages p. 112.

אִי which was doubtless pronounced in the earlier stages of the language īyāth or īyath; for otherwise the י would not have been inserted in writing, as is almost invariably the case in the older inscriptions. In the inscriptions of later date, however, we find את and Plautus heard the word pronounced yth. The Aramaic form seems to be shortened from the Phoenician viz Syriac ܐܝܬ, Chaldee יָת, less correctly יָת״.[1] After the opinion of such an authority the punctuation with P. may fairly be assumed to be incorrect, and that with Q., which is invariably used in the MSS., substituted for it.

According to Merx[2] both the absolute and construct of כל is כָּל or כֹּל, the use of which depends upon the text of the Hebrew original, which is to be attributed to the Massoretic schools. But this is not the case with our MSS. as may be seen from the following examples. 2, 5 כֹּל, where B. and the Hebrew text both read כֹּל. 2, 16 A כָּל, the rest have כֹּל. Hebrew is כָּל. 2, 19 B. and Hebrew כָּל, MSS. כֹּל. 3, 17 B כֹּל. B., A, C, D and the Hebrew כֹּל. 6, 2 B כָּל A, C, D and Hebrew כֹּל. These instances suffice to show that no rule can be fixed to indicate the employment of the two forms. I have, however, noticed that C has Ḥo. throughout except in the following instances כֹּל 35, 6 כֹּל 20, 8 and 45, 8 and 9 and כָּל 47, 17.

Our MSS. always punctuate קֳדָם and this I consider the correct punctuation since the corresponding Syriac word is ܡܢ ܩܕܡ. The Bib. Aram. also supports this reading, since it is קֳדָם and not קֳדָם. Berliner, in his Massorah[3] has קֳדָם as the reading of the Nehardeans and קֳדָם that of the Suraans, whilst the Massorah to Exodus 6, 5 says that קָדְמַי is not the language of the Targum but that of the "Chasdim". In

---

[1] But Schröder justifies either punctuation "Sie wurde ursprünglich mit lautbarem Jod אִית gesprochen, später wurde ijjath, woraus sowohl arab. ijjā als aramäisch *jath, joth* hervorgegangen sind, wie iath, ieth gesprochen und schliesslich mit Unterdrückung auch des a-Lautes, zu ith, yth. Schröder "Die Phönizische Sprache". Halle 1869 p. 213.

[2] Page 31, Note 3 of "Chrestomathia Targumica". [3] p. 64.

spite of this, however, we may safely reject the reading with a full vowel and read קְדָם which is of course קדם in the MSS. As to the word קביל a difference of punctuation exists which can be best understood by tracing the word to its etymology. B. and C לָקֳבֵל 21, 16, A, B and D have לָקֳבֵל. B. and C לְקִבֵיל, A and D לִקְבֵיל! B לָקֳבֵיל 33, 18. All have לְקִבְלֵהוֹן 41, 3. The Syriac forms are ܠܘܩܒܠ, ܠܩܘܒܠܐ ܡܩܒܠ and ܠܡܩܒܠ which may explain the forms לָקֳבֵיל and מְקַבֵּל. Cf. also the Bib. Aram. forms in Daniel 2, 8. קֳבֵיל קֳבֵל and קֳבֵיל are the usual forms we meet with in the Trg. but the readings of A, B and D appear preferable.

Finally, how are we to read the word אִתְיְלִיד which occurs so frequently? We may take 4, 26 as a type. Here B. reads אִיתְיְלִיד, A אִיתְיְלִיד B and D אִתְיְלִיד and C אִתְיְלִיד. The readings of A, B and D are the usual Targumic forms of the Etpeel of ילד whilst C is a Syriasm. Cf. ܐܬܝܠܕ. C invariably has this form.

CHAPTER II.

Examples of the rules contained in the preceding Chapters.

1) Substitution of other vowels for Š. (Cf. Chapter V § 4). (a) P. הֲוָה 4, 2. כֹּל 4, 19. דִי 5, 16. לְסַסְיָן 6, 3, לְבַב וַאֲזַל 10, 2. אֲמַר! 10, 10. (b) Ṣ. קְרִי 23, 9.

2) Substitutions for Še. Compositum (Cp. V, § 5).
 a) Še. mobile.
 α. For Ḥatef P.: תֻשְׁבְּחָא 1, 2. אֲרַע 1, 4. אֲמַר 1, 6. עֲבַד 1, 7. חֲשׁוֹכָא 1, 28.
 β. For Ḥatef S. חֲזָא 24, 60.

b) Še. Quiescens: תְהוֵי 1, 25. הֲוָת 2, 11. נַפְשָׁת 2, 23. אֲרַע 4, 5 [B incorrectly אֲרַע] אַרְעָא 4, 9. הֲוָה 8, 13. אִתְצְדוּ 8, 22. יִשְׁתְלְחוּן 9, 2. הֲוָת 10, 10. (A and D הֲוָת) אַשְׁכַּחְנָא 12, 1. (C אַשְׁכַּחְנָא) אֲרַע 13, 6, הֲוָה 18, 3, (D הֲוָה). הֲוָה 18, 8. פְסִילִין 19, 20. (C פְסִילִין). אֲזַל 21, 16. אֲמַר 30, 36. הֲוָה 31, 32. אַתְרָא 49, 4. B alone has הֲוֵינָן 24, 35.

הָאֱ֗אִין 24, 56. C alone has אֲהִי 42, 1. הֶאֱהִי 45, 26. B and D have בֶּהָאֱהִי 42, 27. B and C have אֲהוּ 44, 34.

In all these instances B. punctuates with Ḥatef P. He punctuates יֱהִי 18, 18 with Ḥatef S.

c) Full vowel: C has אֶהִין 4, 25 (A, B, D write אֲהִין!), B has אֲהִינָא 13, 8 (A, C, D more consistently אֲהִינָא) לְאֲיִהִין 19, 2 (C לְאִיהִין) B has אֲהֹרִין 43, 29. בֲלַא 48, 4. בֲקֵלְדָה 49, 12.

d) Še. Compositum is retained in the following solitary examples. A, B and D have אֶהִין 4, 25, A has עֲבֵדוּד 6, 16. קֳרֵים! 28, 20. אֱחֲרָיָה 36, 2 (B and D הֶאֱחִינָה, C אֱחֱנוּבָה). עֲנָא 36, 2 and D אֱחִירִין 41, 3 and 19.

3) Vowel changes.

a) B. P.: = MSS. Q.[1]

α. Monosyllabic Words and Particles (Cf. Cp. VI, § 3a) בֵּה 2, 4. מֵה 3, 13 (Syriac ܡܘ). בֵּד 13, 3. בֵּה 15, 2 (Syriac ܒܗ). הֲבֵל 15, 16 (Syr. ܗܒܠ). בֵּהּ 15, 16. בֳקֵם 17, 7 (Syriac ܓܡܦܠ). הָרֵב 17, 7 (Syr. ܚܪܒ). בֹּאֱה 17, 11 (Syr. ܐܠܐ). אָן 18, 9 (Hebrew אָן). בֵּהּ 19, 8 (Syr. ܚܠ). בֵּהָה 19, 8. אֱבָא 19, 26. Concerning those words to which the corresponding Hebrew or Syriac forms are not given בֵּה and בֵּהָה are incorrect, according to L. s. v. בֵּהּ is a contraction of בֵּ and בֵּה (time) and this בֵּה is really a shortened form of אֱבָא or, as it is also written מְבָא which latter form may perhaps account for the Q.[2] in the MSS. L. allows בֵּהּ side by side with בֵּה; whilst to justify the Q. of אֱבָא we may compare the Hebrew קָמָה (Exodus 22, 5).

β. Miscellaneous words (VI, 3g) בֹּסֵד 2, 18. אֱהוּדִין 3, 18 (Hebrew אֶפֹד). הָרֵה 3, 21 (Syr.: ܐܦܠ). אֱבֶלָא 9, 12 (Syr.: ܓܠܚܠ). בֵּה 10, 9 (Hebrew עֵמֶר). בֵּרִיד 18, 7 (Syr. ܘܙܢ). בֹּמֵלֵין 27, 23 where, however, L. says we must punctuate סֲמֵלֲרִין. לֱהֶרֵה 42, 13 and 36 &c. where, according to L., the correct reading is בֱהֶרֵה, but when it is noticed that the

---

[1] I write the words as they appear in the MSS.   [2] Cf. Syriac ܡܐ 'what' which is also written ܡܘ.

word לָהּ is merely a contraction of לָא אִית may this fact not justify the Q. which the MSS. read?

b) B. Q. = MSS. P.

α. Vowel of the 2nd Radical of a Verb (VI, 3b) אֶתְקְרִיאַת 3, 7. שְׁוַׁיִוּ¹ 3, 8. דְּחֵילִין 4, 11. דְּמִתְקְרֵא 6, 11. קְטִל 8, 19. וְהַוֵילוֹהִי¹ 14, 15.

β. Absence of Pausal Influence (VI, 3c) בֵּיתֵיהּ 1, 29. בְּשׁוּבָּלֵי 4, 13. חֲדֵית 2, 7. אָמַר 3, 9.

γ. Before the suffixes נִי and הִי (VI, 3d) אֲנָא 11, 4. אַתְקְרִיאַת 5, 29.

δ. Absence of Se. Compositum (VI, 3e) בַּסִּירָא 2, 3. דְּאָמַר 3, 12. אֲסַךְ 3, 13.

c) B. Ṣ. := MSS. H. (VI, 4) שְׁבַק 3, 22. בְּרֵהּ 9, 9. מִטֵּי 9, 20. וְתַלְמִידֵי 11, 2. בְּלֵב 15, 16. מְחִיל 17, 7. דַּלֵב 18, 20. דְּאָכַל 18, 27. In each of these examples (taken from the first 20 Chapters) I have compared the punctuation of the MSS. with that of L. with which it always agrees except קְבִילְתָּא which L. prefers with a S.

d) B. H. = MSS. Ṣ. אֶשְׁקוּל¹ 2, 6. הֲוָה 3, 14. יַחֵת 5, 22. דְּחֵיל 6, 14. אָסִיַא 8, 21. תַּל¹ 9, 13. הַיתַיָא 9, 16. אַלֵצַתָּא 10, 25. בְּרִידַה 11, 3. בְּרִית 11, 7. אַנָא 12, 13. תַּחְלִיד 15, 4. דְּקָדֵם 16, 6. בְּעֵי 16, 7. אַךְ 16, 10. אֱלוּ 18, 13 (A and C here אֲרֵי). עְבַד 18, 17. בְּשַׁלֵם 19, 24. דֵּרֵי 19, 25. דְּשַׁוִּי¹ 19, 33. הַרְפִּית 19, 34.

All these agree with L., with the exception of שַׁמֵּם אֱמַר and שְׁקַעוּהִי which L. punctuates with H. He admits either vowel with בְּלֵבָא and בֵּרִיָּא but prefers H. אָלוּ is as incorrect as B.'s אָבְלֵי since the Imperfect Peal of יְלַד is אֵילַד and the Imperfect Afel is אַלֵד which A and C read. A has some errors, punctuating the following words with S. instead of H. שְׁקַיָא 2, 21. דְּקָרֵי 6, 15. אֲמַר 8, 11 and כְּלַב 18, 19.

e) B. S. = MSS. Ho. (VI, 5) הֲוֵית 2, 16. דְּרֵי 3, 19. תְּלָתָה 5, 1. פָּרִיד 8, 4. בְּעֵיָא 8, 7. שַׁוְיַנִי¹ 8, 17.

---

¹ Likewise Nestorian Syriac has the o sound with Verba ܠܡܕ e. g. ܩܘܡܝ.

הָקְרֵא 8, 22. חָתְלָא 8, 22. דְּרִישִׁיר 9, 5. בָּאִי 15, 17. שָׁבִשָׁוּ 19, 32. Of these L. admits either vowel in the case of הוּרָא תִּילְדַת שֵׁירְבָא קוּרָא but prefers Š. with תְּרוּב דְרִישִׁוּב קְרדוּ.

f) B. Ho. = MSS. Š. טְבִיךְ 4, 7. חָרְלָא 8, 22. בְּלִי 10, 30. טְבִי. Of these L. only punctuates טוּבָךְ with Ho.

g) B. H. = MSS. P. (VI, 7a) כָּסָא 6, 12. הָגְלָה 8, 9. עֲגָלִי 15, 9. A has עָרְחִין 7, 13. For the latter we may compare Syriac ܥܪܚ = with. Of the others L. justifies only רָגְלָה and בְּעַלְבָא.

h) B. P. = MSS. H. (VI, 7b) לְשָׁבְלָא 4, 15. שְׁבְיָה is the Bib. Aram. form. (Dan. 4, 13).

i) B. S. = MSS. P. (VI, 7c) הָצְרַת 6, 7. בְּצַלַם 9, 6. מְצִית 12, 6. קָדְם 19, 9 (D קְדָם) לְצֶרְיָה 19, 31. חָדְיָא 21, 6. Of these קְדָם alone appears to be incorrect, since intransitive Verbs usually have S.[1]

j) B. P. = MSS. S. (VI, 7d). A has עֲצֵין 16, 2 and דָרְיֵן 18, 19 both of which are wrong.

k) B. Ho. = MSS. S. (VI, 7f.) כְּסִדִּי 25, 31, הָסְפִין 44, 23 (C הָסְפִין). A has קְרִי 47, 17 instead of תִלְי. בְּדְרתָך is confirmed by L.; and all of the examples may tend to confirm Derenbourg's statement[2] about the Yemenite Jews viz. that they pronounce the Ho. in the same manner as the Polish Jews.

4) The Vowel of the Imperfect (VI, 6) דְּלִשְׁתְחִית 4, 15. אָכֵת 6, 7. אָכֵב 14, 23 (C אָכֵב). אָכֵהִית 13, 15. אָכֵב 16, 2 (C אָכֵב). אָחֵי 17, 8 (C אָהֵב). אֶשְׁתִיו 19, 20 (B אִשְׁתִי). In those examples with initial א the P. stands for S. which would be the Sbl. punctuation.

5) Interchange of Še. and full Vowel.

a) MSS. Še. = B. P. (VI, 8a) הָשְׁעְבִירוּ 12, 5. אָחִין 13, 8. אָרִיחַת 14, 22. הַשְׁאֵף 19, 7.

b) MSS. Še. = B. Q. טְרִיד 4, 7. אָחִי 4, 9. קָכֵד 4, 10. הָלְבִין 6, 20. חוּר 9, 23. לְהָבָא 10, 13. אָרְדָאי 10, 18.

[1] This is however not always the case "Non solum intransitiva velut קְם sed etiam transitiva velut אֱכָל Dan. 2, 10, שְׁפַל Dan. 3, 27 in Zere terminari possunt" Baer: (l. c.) P. LIX. [2] Manuel du Lecteur p. 511.

אָרִיב 14, 16. כְּלָא 15, 17. לְבַלָּא 16, 7. בְּיָקָא 16, 8. אָקְמֵי 17, 21. (*D* אָקֵם). Of these חזי and כוי being Preterites Peal of Verbs have Še. correctly. In מלאכא קדמי עדיר and אחין the Še. mobile corresponds to the Še. compositum with which these words may be punctuated in the Sbl. system; but the Afel forms אריב and אקם seem to be incorrect with Še.

c) B. = S.; MSS. = Še. (VI, 8c) אֶבְלָאי 18, 16. בְּלִשָּׁתִין 10, 20. אֶלָּבוּ 12, 3. אָלְהִין 15, 4. אֶבִילֵי 18, 31. All these are truer to the character of the Aramaic language whilst B.'s forms are Hebraisms. אלהין alone appears rather doubtful, but, according to Merx [1], the Še. is justified by Buxtorf in his Dictionary.

6) Orthographical Variations (VII, 1e) *C* has נְבלֵה (without final א) 19, 24. Occasionally the punctuation of the MSS. seems to be in an unsettled state. Thus in 13, 12 *B* has הַיִב and הַיַב in the same verse; whilst *D* has הַיָב and הַיָב. The correct reading is הַיָב. Elsewhere, *C* appearing to be in doubt which is the correct punctuation writes דְגַלְבִין! L.[2] admits either vowel but prefers H.

The same MS. has אִירִין immediately followed by יָרִין in 30, 31, but the P. is here correct since it stands for S. in the Sbl. system. We occasionally meet with forms which remind us of the Sbl. vocalization. Thus *B* has אֲרָיִב 24, 50 and אַרְיִב 27, 25. *A*, *B* and *C* write אֲבָהָתִין 28, 15 (but *D* אֲבָהָתִין) *A* and *D* have בְּדִילָא 3, 19 which we may take as a Hebraism; the others more correctly בְּדִילָא. The MSS. read הַחְלָא and הַרִינָא but הַחְלָא and בְּדִילָא would be more correct forms since in Syriac these words are written with ܚܕܐ ܡܢ. MSS. read בִּהָּ. 23, 15. B. has בִּי. L. says that in this word and in אֶאֱ the suffix of the 1st Person Singular is wanting [3]. In 14, 10 the MSS. imitate

---

[1] l. c. s. v. [2] l. c. s. v.

[3] So also in Christian Palestinian Aramaic the suffix of the First Person Singular is wanting in the word ܐܒܐ which = ܐܒܝ "my father" (cf. Nöldeke's Article in the ZDMG. l. c. p. 514).

the Hebrew original reading בִּדִין בֵּית but Path^{s}egen reads as B. viz בֵּירִין and this is also L.'s reading. The word being of common Gender may perhaps assume either the Masculine or Feminine ending in its plural. *A, B, C* read בֵּסָא but *D* has בֵּסָף which is closer to the Hebrew original. *B, C, D* read אִחָא 18, 6 but *A* אִיתָאִי which latter reading is preferred by Berliner[1], Landauer[2], Levy[3], Path^{s}egen[4] but Adler[5] prefers אִחָא as *B, C* and *D* have. In the same verse *A* has פָּאן, *B* and *D* דָּאן, *C* כָּאן whilst B. writes סָאִן which, says L.[6] is the correct form. 18, 15 *A* has חֲרִיבָה, *B, C* and *D* חָרִיבת. *A*'s reading, says the author of the Path^{s}egen is the Trg. of צְחִיקָה. 18, 21, *C* אַדרִין, B. אָרְיָן, *B'*, *A* and *D* אֲדֵר. Both forms אָדְרִין and אָרְיִן are allowed by L. but the latter corresponds to the Syriac form. 19, 9 *A, B, C* קָרִב, B. and *D* קָרִיב. L.[7] gives the latter form, but Merx[8] the former. (V. Pt. II, II, 3 i, note). Bib. Aram. קְרֵב Dan. 3, 26. 19, 13. In this verse B. gives the better reading, having קָבִילְתֵחִי which is likewise given by L. All the MSS. read קָבִילתֵחִין here. B. and C read חֲשִׁיבִין 50, 20 whilst *A, B* and *D* have חָשְׁבִין. L. has the former reading. We may compare the Arabic in which حَسَبَ = to number and حَسِبَ = to think. וַחֲקִיפ 19, 15 which is the reading given by the MSS. is more correct than B.'s text וְרָחִיקוּ when compared with the Syriac ܚܣܢ although L. s. v. mentions both forms. In 42, 23 *A, B* and *D* write שָׁצֵה whilst *C* and B. give נְצָה. We may perhaps compare the former reading with the Arabic verb شَصَى. Likewise the P. in the word אַשִּיבֵב 19, 20 is a better reading than B.'s אָשֵׁיזֵב although L. gives this form. We may compare the Syriac ܐܫܬܘܙܒ although I am informed that here we have a word borrowed from the Assyrian which has u^{s}tîzib or u^{s}têzib. MSS. כְּסִבֵּהּ 19, 21 which both Landauer

---

[1] l. c. p. 7.   [2] Massorah s. v.   [3] s. v.   [4] To this verse.
[5] חִנְּתֵיהּ לִבּוּ a. l.   [6] s. v.   [7] s. v.   [8] "Chrestomathia Targumica". s. v.

and Berliner give as a Nehardean reading in their Massorahs, and which is evidently intended to imitate the Hebrew original which has הֵקִים. B. reads לְהַקָמָה. 9, 22 B. בְּרַיִ, *A*, *B* and *D* בְּרַיָּא, *C* בְּרַיָּה. The correct reading, according to L. is בְּרָיָא. B. adds the final א in his notes. 20, 4, B. וַאֲזַי. B. אֵזַי, *A*, *C* and *D* אֱדַי. Perhaps the best reading is אֱדַי. Cf. Syriac ܗܝܕܝܢ¹. 20, 7 B. לְמִקְרֵי *A*, *C* and *D* לְמִקְרָא and *B* has לְמִקְרָא לֹא! of course *B*.'s reading is absurd. Of the others *A*, *C* and *D* retain the more classical form of which לְמִקְרָ is merely a contraction. Cf. Syriac ܠܡܩܪܐ. On the other hand B.'s reading עֲנַיִן in 20, 10 appears preferable to עָנַיָּא which the MSS. give, although L. also gives a final א² (s. v.). But the reading of the MSS. is again preferable in הֻבְהָלָה 24, 2 and not as B. reads הִתְבְּהִלוּ³ and again in אָזְדַּרְבְּלוּ 24, 14 and in אִשְׁתַּכַּח 24, 43; B.'s readings being אַזְדַּרְבְּלוּ and אִשְׁתְּכַח. In 24, 60 B. has חַיָּא, *A* חָיֵא, *B* חָיֵי, *C* חַיָּא and *D* הַיָּא of which *D* is the most correct, although the א is superfluous. Cf. the Syriac form ܚܝܐ. 25, 25 B. פָּסוּק. *A*, *B* and *D* פָּסֵק, *C* פְּסוּק. L. confirms the first-mentioned reading. B. is again more correct in reading אַשְׁפַּז 26, 3. MSS. read אַשְׁפָּז. *C* invariably reads שָׂרָבָא⁴. The other MSS., more correctly, שָׂרְבָא. Cf. the Bib. Aram. שֵׁגָל Daniel 5, 10 and the corresponding Syriac forms ܫܓܠܐ. *A* has the uncontracted form אַוָּז 27, 32. Cf. Syriac ܐܘܙ. B. תַּהֲוֵי 27, 40. MSS. תֶּהֱוֵה which L. gives as the correct Imperfect of הֲוָה.

The MSS. are again preferable in the same verse, giving יְהֹודְעוּן, whilst B. has יְהֹדְעוּ, although the latter form is given by L. The MSS. again have the more correct form in

---

¹ And also Biblical Aramaic הֵדַיִן Ezra 2, 9.   ² But the Q. is justifiable according to Bib. Aram. cf. Daniel 5, 22 עֲנַיִן.   ³ But Baer in his Paradigms of Biblical Aramaic forms gives a similar form to that of Berliner l. c.) p. XXII.   ⁴ Dalman asserts that short L occasionally occurs where we should expect Še. and he instances the word יוֹם and compares Hieronymus' transcription of בְּיוֹם to biom (p. 62 of his Grammar). Cf. also *C*'s readings of לְמִקְרָא 19, 20 and אָזְדַּרְבְּלוּ 12, 1 and *B*'s reading חָיֵי 24, 60.

חֲזִית. 30, 27 and not as B. חֲזֵית which is a Hebraism. B and B. have וִירִידָא 30, 39 but A, D and C יְרִידִין. The Hebrew is יַחְדָּו. A, B and D have בְּלֵילְיָא 31, 2 whilst B. and C give לֵילְיָא. The correct form, according to L., is בְּלֵילְיָא. B, C, D שַׁבְטַיָּא 31, 26, A שִׁבְטַיָּא, B. שַׁבְטַיָּא. The first mentioned reading appears preferable since L. punctuates the word with H. and it is in the construct state. A and B חֵיוַת 31, 27, C and D חֵיוַת. B. חֵיוָתָא. L. writes חוית¹. B. and B are correct in reading יִסַּךְ 31, 49 which reading is also supported by L., although Pathšegen prefers יֹסֵךְ which C reads. A and D (incorrectly) יֵיסֵךְ. A is again at fault in בֵּר 32, 14, the fuller form בְּרָא being preferable. Cf. the Syriac ܛܠܐ. 33, 12 A, B מִיל, B., C and D נְמִיל. Pathšegen also נְמִיל. Our Editions of Raši's Commentary to the Pentateuch give his reading of this passage as מִיל, but according to Luz. 'Oheb Ger' and L. Raši also gave the correct reading נְמִיל which was only altered by ignorant copyists who strove to bring the Trg. into harmony with Raši's interpretation of the word מִסְכָּה. 33, 14 B. כַּאֲדָדָא, MSS. כַּחֲדָא. Pathšegen and L. read as B. but it may be remarked that the words are synonyms, and hence either reading is allowable. C's reading דָּוָי 'my grief' 35, 18 is a more literal rendering of the Hebrew אוֹנִי than is that of B. A, B and D who write דָּוֵי 'grief'. 35, 17. The MSS. reading תַּדְחֲלִין is more correct than that of B. who has תְּדַחֲלִין. L. gives the same form as that of the MSS. 37, 23 B. בְּאוּנְדְרֵיהּ, MSS. בְּאוּנְדְרֵיהּ. The Hebrew text is בְּתֻמּוֹ. B. seems to be a Hebraism. L. gives a similar reading to that of the MSS.

39, 23 B. חֲוַי, MSS. הֲוָה. The latter reading is again preferable and is given by L. We may compare the Syriac form ܗܘܐ. 41, 25 A (incorrectly) עֲדִיד, B, C and D בְּהִיד. B. עֲדִיד which is a Hebraism. Cf. Syriac ܥܬܝܕ. 43, 33 MSS. בְּמִשְׁלְמֵי which Berliner, in his Massorah², following Luz. Lan-

---

¹ We may also compare the form with final ה which occasionally occurs in Biblical Aramaic. Cf. חֱזֵיְתָה Dan. 2, 41.   ² p. 117.

dauer and the בְּסִירִין הַתַּרְגּוּם¹ all declare a false reading. B. בְּרַבּוּתֵיהּ. 45, 4 A, B, C קָדְלֵי, D קָדְלֵי, B. קֳדָם. D's reading is here the best, and is confirmed by reference to the Chrestomathies of Merx and Levy². 46, 29. The MSS. give the curious reading הַהִיְתוֹהִי but since the Hebrew has the Singular form כְּרַבוּתֵהּ the reading of B. who gives רְבוּתֵיהּ appears preferable. 49, 12 B., A, B and D הֲוֵי, C הֲוָה. Both L. and Merx prefer the reading of C.

7) Grammatical Variations. A. The Nominal States.

α) Absolute and Emphatic (VIII, 1a, α). C, D and B. לִיהוּדָאֵי דָּר 7, 2, A and B הָבֵא. Hebrew is עֲתִידָה. A reads אֲנָשׁ 8, 3; 12, 6; 13, 6. The rest אָלֵּא-אֵל. The Hebrew in each case has הָאָרֶץ. B., C and D הָבֵל, A and B בָּהָתָא 15, 18. Text is מִיהַב. 18, 14, MSS. כֹּלָּא. B. לְמִירְדָא. The Hebrew is לְמִלָּא. 20, 4 B. and C גְּבַר (גֻּב), A, B, D בָּאלֵ. Hebrew הָאִישׁ. 21, 2 A לְיוֹם. B., B, C and D יוֹמָא. Hebrew לַמִּשְׁפָּט. 19, 26 B., B and C חַיִּין, A and D בָּהַלָּהּ. Hebrew הִיא. 28, 17 B. אֻרְיָן, MSS. אָל. Hebrew בְּקִרְיָה. 31, 39 B הַתְבִּיר B., A, D and C בָּהִיתָא. Hebrew הָבֵר. 33, 20 C הָדָא. B., A, B and D בָּהָדָא. Hebrew בְּדָא. 34, 10 B. and C סְתִים (Pathsegen likewise). A, B and D בְּתַמָּה. 37, 31 B. and C בָּאִישׁ. A, B and D בִּישׁ. Hebrew שֻׁלָּי. 38, 2 B. and C בְּבָב, A and D לֵב, B בָּאָב. Hebrew בְּלֵב. (For variant reading, see Part II; II, 7j).

β) Absolute and Construct (VIII, 1a, β). 2, 9 and 17 A and B הַהֵיכָל. D and B. הֵיכָל (L., likewise). C missing.

(B) Number (VIII, 1b). Several variations are noticeable with the verb היה. In 1, 14 A has יְהִי בֶּאֱרָאָ whilst B., B, C and D give יְהִי יְהוֹן. A's reading is probably based upon the reading of the Hebrew text יְהִי בְּאֶרְאֵר but it must be remarked as Luz. has already pointed out in his

---

¹ Contained in Adler's Edition of the Targum.
² Cf. also Daniel 3, 26 קָדָם.

אהב גר that it is contrary to the custom of the Aramaic language to place a verb in the Singular whose subject is in the Plural, even though the Verb precedes the Subject. In the Hebrew and Arabic languages this construction is permissible and is frequently employed. MSS. הֲוָה B. הֲוֹן 1, 29; 9, 15 and 47, 24. In each of these cases the Hebrew is יִהְיֶה. In 47, 24 B.'s reading is the only correct one, but the reading given by the MSS., may perhaps be justified in the other two examples, through the subjects being collective; indeed עַמָּא 9, 15 may be taken as Singular. B. לְהוֹן MSS. לֵיהּ 9, 26. The Hebrew is לוֹ. B.'s reading is given in Berliner's Massorah Parva but the other reading is more literal. Some confusion appears to exist whether to use an adjective or the Plural of a noun when describing nations. Thus *A*, *B*, *D* עַמְמַיָּא 10, 18 (B. and *C* עַמְמַיָּה). *A*, *B* and *C* עַמְמַיָּה 24, 3 (B. and *D* עַמְמַיָּא) B., *A*, *C* and *D* עַמְמַיָּא 24, 37 (*B* עַמְמַיָּה). B., *A*, *C* and *D* בְּעַמְמַיָּא 34, 30 (*B* בְּעַמְמַיָּה). B., *A*, *C* and *D* חוֹרָאָה 30, 21 (*B* חִוָּרָה). In 16, 12. *A*, *D* and *C* (text) have the incorrect reading יְהֵא בָּרִיךְ *B* and *C* (margin) צָרִיכִין חוֹן which is also given by B. and confirmed by L. 17, 13, *A* וְלִידֵי וּבְנֵי. *B*, *C*, *D* and B. הֲלִידֵי וּבְנָךְ. Now, although the sense of the whole passage might justify a plural here, still the form of the original being Singular confirms the latter reading, which is likewise given by L. 21, 12 *A* וְתִקְרֵי, *B*, *C*, *D* וְהִקְרוּן. The Hebrew text וְקָרָא is Singular the Subject of the Verb being עַם but we require a Plural in the Trg. since the Subject is בְּנוֹי. 25, 26 *B* (incorrectly) יִהְיֶה *A*, *C*, *D* and B. יְהֵי. The original is יִרְדּוּ. *B* is again incorrect in reading בֵּירָא 26, 15 which should be בֵּירָה as the other MSS. and B. give. 27, 15 *A* (incorrectly) דִּכְרַיָּא. *B*, *C*, *D* and B. דִּכְרַיָּה which L. confirms. 27, 27 B. הֲוָה MSS. הֲוֵה. 27, 36 *A*, *B* בְּכֵן, *C*, *D* and B. בָּכֵן. The latter is likewise given both by L. and the author of the Path*egen; still it is strange why we should read בְּכֵן in 27, 12 the Hebrew of both passages being

בְּקָרָ. 27, 39 B. בְּקָרֵי which is also given by the Path-šegen. MSS. have בְּקָרֵי. Hebrew is בְּקָשָׁה. Berliner mentions the Variant reading in his Massorah, but offers no comment upon it. 30, 39 B. and C אֲבָדָא. A, B and D אֲבָדָן. We require the Plur. Fem. here, hence אֲבָדָן is more correct. 31, 26, 43 and 50. B. בְּמִי, MSS. בְּמִי. Hebrew בְּמִי; hence the reading given by the MSS. is correct. 31, 43 B., B and D בִי. A and C בִי. The Hebrew being אֲנִי, the first reading is preferable. 34, 5. B. יְהִירִין. MSS. יְהִירָן, Pathšegen supports the reading given by B., but since the Hebrew is בִּקְרָהוּ we should expect בְּהִירָא as the MSS. 34, 24 B (incorrectly) בְּרֵהוֹן which appears to refer the suffix both to Šehem and Hamor. The other MSS. have בְּרֵהוֹן which corresponds to the Hebrew בְּרָם. 37, 4 A (incorrectly) אֲבוּהִי. The other MSS. אֲבִיהוֹן which corresponds to the Hebrew אֲבִיהֶם. The correct Trg. of בְּנוֹת 39, 5 is בְּנָתָא which all the MSS. have. B. reads בְּנָתָא (plural) which is incorrect. 41, 36 B יִשְׂרָאֵל, A, C, D and B. יִשְׂרָאֵל. Either reading may perhaps be justified since עַם is a collective Noun, but the Singular is preferable. 46, 20 B. and B אֲגָרֵיהּ. C אֲגָרֵיהּ. A and D אֲגָרָה. Hebrew שְׂכַר אִשָּׁה. A and D are correct κατὰ σύνεσιν. C is wrong. Landauer supports B.'s reading in his Massorah. 47, 30. B., B and C (incorrectly) אַחָאָה. A and D אַחָאָה which is also given by L. The Hebrew text has אָחִיו. 50, 9 B., B (original reading) and C סְבִיבוֹי. A, D and B (corrected reading) סְבִיבוֹ. Hebrew is בְּכֹל.

(C) Gender (VIII, 1c). A and B הֲוָה B. and D הֲווֹ 1, 26. The subject is אֱנָשׁ which being of common gender, perhaps admits of either form; but L. reads as B.

B. בְּכִרִי, MSS. בְּכֵן 4, 10. Hebrew is הָרִים which however refers to הַר whilst the Trg. refers to טוּר which is feminine and hence the reading of the MSS. is more correct. Pathšegen notices this variant reading and seems to expect that of the MSS. B. הֲוָה, A, B, D הֲוָה, C (incorrectly) הֲ 14, 7. The Hebrew is הוּא which agrees with עִיר but אָבוּהִי

is masculine in Aramaic and hence B.'s reading is the correct one.

A, *B* and *D* הֵלָא, B. and *C* הֵלָה 15, 9. L. has the latter reading but points out that the Peshitta of this passage is ܚܡܪܐ ܘܐܬܐ.

16, 2 *A* (incorrectly) בְּנֵיהּ, the rest have בְּלָהּ. 19, 8 B., *A* and *C* דְּלֵיתִין, *B* דְּלֵילָן, *D* דְּלֵעֵילָן. The subject being בֵּן *D* is of course a mistake. 20, 9 *A* (incorrectly) בְּעִירָךְ; the rest have בְּעִירִין. *A*, *B* and *D* are incorrect in having דִּין 20, 13 since טִיבְלָךְ is feminine. B. and *C* read דָּא. *B* is incorrect in reading הָדָא 19, 13 since אָתְרָא is masculine. Rest have הָדֵין. The Hebrew in each case is זֶה and this may perhaps account for the error of *A*, *B* and *D* in 20, 13. 21, 30 B. and *C* הָדָא, *A*, *B* and *D* הָדֵין. Since בִּירָא is given by L. as of common gender either reading may be justified; but *B*'s reading הָדָא in 24, 58 and *A*'s הָדָא in 25, 30 are both evidently incorrect. The fact of בִּירָא being of common gender may again justify both readings in 26, 20 in which verse *A* reads עֲמִירָה whilst B., *B*, *C* and *D* give שְׁמָּה. 27, 42 *A* and *C* (incorrectly) בִּירָה, B., *B* and *D* הֵלָא. 29, 3 B. מַשְׁקִין, which L. also reads. MSS. מַשְׁקָן. Pathshegen also as B. who gives the proper gender, the subject being the shepherds. 30, 37 *A* and *D* רְטִיבִין, *B*, *C* and B. רְטִיבָן. So also L. and Pathshegen, but since חוּטְרִין is of common gender we may take either reading as correct. 30, 40 all the MSS. have שָׂרִיבִינָן which is the proper reading, B. has עָרִיבִינָן which is certainly incorrect. 30, 43 *A* סַגְיָאִין, B., *B*, *C* and *D* סַגְיָאן. *A*'s reading is more correct, עָאן being masculine. 31, 10 B., *C* and *D* הַסֹּלְקִין, *A* and *B* הַסֹּלְקָן which is a mistake since אָדְשָׁא is masculine. *A* is again incorrect in reading וְסַגְדִין 37, 7 and אַתְיָן 41, 3. In both instances we require the feminine. 39, 5 *B* תִּהוּ, B., *A*, *C*, *D* יְהוּ. *B* is the correct reading; the other imitates the Hebrew Idiom. 41, 20 *B* and *C* read אִינּוּן but the 2nd time the word occurs in the verse אִינּוּן. B., *A* and *D* have both times אִינּוּן which is correct since the first one refers to תְּהֹמָא and the second

one to שְׁבַבְלָא and both these words are feminine. 48, 4
All the MSS. read אַגְשִׁישִׁין here, whilst B. has אַגְשָׁרִין
which reading is defended in Berliner's Massorah[1] referring,
as it does, to the feminine בְּרִיתָה. Landauer writes to the
same effect in his Massorah[2]. But, it may be remarked,
that יַד is also sometimes masculine. Cf. Targum Jonathan
to Isaiah 13, 7 כָּל יְדָא תִתְרַשְּׁלִין.

(D) The Conjugations of the Verb.

α. Peal and Pael (VIII, 2a, α). A גָּבַר, B., B, C and
D דָּחִי 8, 4. B. שִׁירֵךְ, MSS. שִׁישֵׁךְ 27, 27; 29, 13; 50, 1.
A גּוֹבַר, B., B, C, D דָּחִי 31, 20. B שַׁוִּי, B., A, C, D
שַׁוִּי 31, 34. A, B, C דָּחִי, D דָּחִי, B. יְבַעֵר 31, 40. B.
יְצַבַּר, MSS. צָבָר 35, 4. A and B שַׁבְלָא, B. and C שַׁבְלָא, D
שַׁחְלָא 42, 16. Aramaic requires a Pael here. A and B perhaps
a Hebraism. 43, 4 B (incorrectly) נְזַבֵּן = we shall sell, it
should be נְזַבֵּן we shall buy, which is given by A, C, D
and B. 43, 7 MSS. שְׁאֵל־. B. שָׁאֵל just like the Hebrew
text. L. has the same orthography as the MSS, but I think
שְׁאַל־ would be a preferable punctuation, since L. gives no
Pael of this root. 45, 24 A (incorrectly) נְשַׁבֵּי. B., B, C
and D נְשַׁבֵּי. 50, 21 B. נְגֵיב, MSS. נְגִיב. Although L.
mentions both these forms as Pael of נגב still the only
correct Aramaic form of the Pael is that given by the MSS.

β. Peal and Afel (VIII, 2a, β). B (incorrectly) נְשַׁבֵּי
12, 13, A, C and D נַשְׁבֵּי, B. נַשְׁבֵּי. The latter reading is
supported by the authority of L. B. אֵילֵי, B, D אֲזִל, A,
C אוֹזִיל 18, 13. Of these three readings the Afel is certainly incorrect. Of the two other forms given B.'s is
preferable, although the correct form is אָזֵל. B אֲזֵל, B.,
A, C and D אֲזֵל 32, 23. L. as B.

γ. Peal and Etpeel, Etpaal or Ettafal (VIII, 2a, γ). B.
גַּוְזֵי and גַּוְזֵי. MSS. אִתְגְּזַר and אִתְגְּזַר 17, 26 and 27. (Vide
VII, 1i). B. הֶקְבֵּר 25, 23 (Peal) whilst the MSS. read

---

[1] l. c. p. 78.   [2] s. v.

חִתְפַּל (Etpaal). In this instance, we may perhaps take either reading, since both give good sense, the Etpaal having a reflective sense.

δ) Pael and Afel (VIII, 2a, δ). *A, B* הֵסְגִּיתִ. B., *C* and *D* הִסְגֵּית 3, 18. The latter reading is also given by L. B. אַגְשִׁיתִי, *A, C, D* אַגְשִׁית, *B* אַשְׁוִית 13, 16. Both the Pael and Afel forms give sense here. Pael = I have made numerous, Afel = I have made equally numerous. B. has an inferior Aramaic form.

ε) Etpeel and Etpaal (VIII, 2a, ε). 7, 11 *A, D* אִתְאֲמַרָא, B., *B* and *C* אִתְאֲמָרָא. L. also reads Etpaal, but in the Syriac language the Etpeel (and not Etpaal) is the conjugation in use[1]. 8, 2 MSS. הֶאֱמַרִי, B. אִתְאֲמָרוּ. L. again has Etpaal but according to Bernstein-Kirsch, the Etpeel is the usual Syriac conjugation. 10, 9 and 27, 13 MSS. תֶּאֱמַר, B. יִתְאֲמַר. Although L. again has the Etpaal here, he gives Etpeel = Etpaal, so that MSS. may again be justified. 14, 15 *A, D* אִתְגְּלִיאָ, *B* הָאִתְגְּלִיג, *C* הִתְגְּלִיאָ, B. יִתְגַּלַּף. L. here reads as *A* and *D* but again notices Etpeel = Etpaal. *C* has an impossible form. 29, 26 B., *B* and *C* מִתְעֲבִיד, *A* and *D* יִתְעֲבִיד. The Hebrew is יֵעָשֶׂה. Berliner, in his Massorah[2] says that the Hebrew Imperfect is here to be rendered by the Aramaic Participle, but L. gives the same reading as *A* and *D* which thus appear to give the most correct reading. 31, 24 and 29 and 42, 24. *A, B* and *D* אִסְתְּמַר, *C* and B. אִסְתְּמַר. L. has the Etpaal form. 34, 7 *A, B* and *D* אִתְחַסִּיאוּ. B. יִתְחַנְסָאוּ, *C* הִתְחַסִּיס. The latter reading will be considered when the Variae Lectiones will be treated of. Of the other two readings, the Etpaal appears to be more correct, since this form is given by L. 45, 1, On the other hand L. confirms the MSS. reading of Etpeel here. B. has אִירְיְדַע, MSS. אִתְידַע.

(E) The Tenses of the Verb (VIII, 2 b, α).

α) Perfect and Imperfect B. דְּיִשְׁתְּחֵינֵיהּ 4, 14, *B, C* and *D*

---

[1] v. Bernstein-Kirsch l. c. s. v.   [2] l. c. p. 25.

הָשְׁתַּכַחַת, *A* has שְׁכִיחִין. Of these *A* is incorrect since the Hebrew מָצָא could not be translated by a Perfect. Of the other forms given L. prefers the Afel (Cf. VIII, 2a, β). *A* יַחֲוֵה, B., *B, C, D* יְחַוֵי 9, 14. *A* is here incorrect.

β) Perfect and Present (VIII, 2b, β). *A, C, D* and B. יָדְעָא, *B* יְדַע 4, 9. The Hebrew is יָדַע to which *B* agrees in form; but the Massorahs of both Berliner and Landauer give יָדְעָא as the correct form here. MSS. יָדְעָא, B. אָרְחֲבַד 23, 13. There is no corresponding word in the Hebrew text, but the sense seems to be present and hence B. is perhaps preferable. Landauer notices this variant reading. 27, 14 MSS. דְּחִילִין, B. דְּחִילוּ. Text is אֲנָא and therefore the MSS. give the better text. 29, 5 B. הֵיתֵיתִי, MSS. הַיְתָיוּן The Hebrew is הֵיתָיוּ which is again Perfect in form but Present in meaning. Pathšegen reads Participle which he says the Aramaic idiom requires. So L. although he also mentions the reading of the MSS. similarly in 44, 27. 29, 26 see above under Etpaal and Etpeel. 30, 39 B. אִתְיְהִיב, *A* and *C* אִתְיְהִיב, *B* and *D* אִתְיְהִב. The Hebrew is נִתַּן. B. has the correct reading although some confusion exists here between the Perfect and Participle. In 30, 31 and 41 and in 31, 8 the Participle is used; but in 31, 10 again Perfect. 30, 41 *B* שַׁוִּי, B., *A, C, D* שַׁוִּיו. L. reads וְשַׁוִּי according to the Aramaic idiom, although looking at the Hebrew שָׂם we might perhaps have expected the Preterite. 31, 6 MSS. יָהֲבִין, B. יָהֲבִין Merx, in the Dictionary to his Chrestomathia Targumica regards the manuscript reading as a vulgarism, and Luz. in his Oheb Ger also gives the participial form as correct. 31, 8 B. יַלְדִין, MSS. יָלְדִין. The Hebrew is again Perfect. 41, 1 *A, D* חֶלְמָא, B., *B* and *C* חֲלַם. The Hebrew text is חָלַם but L. has the reading חֲלַם which is also supported by Pathšegen, according to the use of the Aramaic language. 41, 45 B. דָּרֶךְ, *A, B* and *D* דְּגָלֵי, *C* (just as the Hebrew) גְּבַר רָזִין. L. reads as B. "a man who reveals secrets". The best reading appears to be that of *C*, who does not attempt to give a rendering of the name. Besides it is by no means certain that these two Egyptian words mean "revealer of secrets" (as the Trg. and Pešitta). Gesenius[1] explains the title to signify "saviour of the age" in the Egyptian language[2]. 44, 15 B. and C יְדַעְהִי, A, B and D הֻדַעְתִּי. Here the Hebrew יָדַעְתִּ has the sense of a Perfect and hence the reading of A, B and D is better. 47, 22 A וַאֲבֵלוּ, B., B, C and D אַבְלִין. The Hebrew text is וַיֹּאכְלוּ and the sense of the passage appears to require a Past Tense and therefore the reading of A is preferable. It may be noticed that in the instances quoted above the MSS. follow the Hebrew text literally, but B. gives us the sense of the Hebrew text.

γ) Imperfect and Present (VIII, 2b, γ) A, B and D יוּבָל (Imperfect), B. and C יָבֵל (Present) 48, 10. The latter reading is perhaps better. The Hebrew is יוּבַל.

(F) Additions (IX, 2). A and D read בְּמֵימְרֵיה before כַּלָּיה 7, 16. C inserts the same word on the margin. This version represents the opinion of those who wish to interpret the words וַיִּסְגוֹר יי בַּעֲדוֹ figuratively, to denote generally that the Divine protection encompassed and preserved him. 14, 12 C has כָּל before קִנְיָנֵיה probably confusing this verse with the preceding. 18, 25 A, B, D have הֻדַעְתִּין which is pointed out by B.[3] as an incorrect reading and so also the insertion of לֹא before כֻלֵּה which A has in the same verse. Adler and Pathšegen also both object to this reading since the Targumist always avoids irreverent language when speaking of the

---

[1] l. c. s. v.   [2] The LXX has ψονθομφανήχ, Siegfried and Stade in their "Hebräisches Wörterbuch zum alten Testamente (Leipzig, 1893) give צפנת פענח "Egyptian title of Joseph. According to G. Steindorff, Zeitschr. f. ägypt. Sprache u. Altertumskunde XXVII, 41 f. — es spricht der Gott und er lebt". Jerome renders "salvator mundi" but according to Rosellini the name means sustentator vitae, support or sustainer of life. The Targum version seems to be the popular Jewish interpretation. Cf. Josephus Ant. II, 6. V. Keil and Delitzsch, Commentary to the Pentateuch, Vol. I, p. 35. Translated by Martin. (Edinburgh 1874).   [3] l. c. p. 221.

Deity. But, since it is a more literal translation of the original Hebrew the manuscript reading seems preferable. 19, 34 B. רֵישָׁא, *A*, *B* and *D* בְּרֵישׁ, *C* בְּרֵישָׁא. The Hebrew is אֵשׁ. L. seems to know of no reading בְּרֵישׁ but Landauer in his Massorah[1] gives both readings and also explains the ב of בְּרֵישִׁי as standing for an accusative of time. The best reading would then be בְּרֵישָׁא. I do not know why the suffix of the 1st Person Singular is affixed to this word. 23, 8. The MSS. insert אִיתּ before רְשׁוּ which improves the sense and follows the original. 24, 67 *C* has דְּבֵּיהּ אִימֵיהּ before והוּא thus first giving the literal translation before proceeding to the Hag. rendering which follows and which may perhaps with advantage be deleted. 25, 8 *B* has יְלִידִין after כְּסַף. Since *D* has the same word on the margin, we may perhaps take this word as a gloss which has crept into the text of *B*. 26, 26 B., *C* and *D* דְּחַמְיֵיהּ, *A* and *B* בְּחַמְיֵיהּ. L. rejects the latter reading which is against the spirit of the Aramaic idiom. We must then read, either דְּחַמְיֵיהּ or בַּחֲמֵיהּ which have exactly the same significations, the ב being part of the word and not a preposition. 31, 13 MSS. בְּבֵיתּ. B. בֵּיתּ. Hebrew בֵיתּ. The sense justifies the reading of the MSS. and although Pathšegen also reads בֵּית he seemed to have expected the reading בְּבֵית and hence we may take the reading of the MSS. as correct. 31, 48 *B* incorrectly inserts הִיא before כָּל. 42, 28 *A* has בְּבֵם before יוֹמֵי but the scribe was probably looking at the preceding verse. 34, 14 *B* has דִי before בְּגַוֵית. 39, 6 *B* and *C* insert דִי before כָּל. 43, 29 *B* has יה before שִׁווּהִי. It may be noticed that these insertions, the majority of which appear to be incorrect are confined to *B* and *C*. Finally, I have to mention a few Prepositions which are here and there added.

לְ is added by *C* in לְכָאן 17, 5 and לְכָאן 17, 10, *A*, *C* and *D* have לְכֵן 29, 3. *A* has לְאַבָּא and לְבִין 45, 8 which reading is rejected by Pathšegen. *A*, *B* and *D* לְשָׁאוּל 49, 8

---

[1] l. c. s. v.

which Merx also reads. ו is added by the MSS. וּבְבָבֶל
9, 10 which is against the Hebrew text and in יְהִירִין 33, 13
which follows the Hebrew original. בּ is added in מֵהַמְנֵהּ
26, 26 by *A* and *B* but this has already been noticed as a
faulty reading. *A*, *D* add אֱנָשׁ before בָּרִיא 45, 8 and this is
really the sense of the passage. The same reading is given
in Adler's edition of the Trg. The MSS. add an initial ד
in דְלִבְבֵהּ 15, 18 which *A* and *C* read. *A* has דְאָכַר 20, 5
and again דְדַחֵל 24, 22. *B* (incorrectly) הֲשַׁלְטֵהּ 35, 5. All
the MSS. read דְלֵילְיָא 40, 1. *A* has דְשִׁלְטֵי 42, 6. *C* and *D*
have דְבַצְבְּעֵהּ 45, 13. All MSS. read וְהוֹדָא 46, 1. *B* and
C give דְּכֹל 50, 13. בּ is added by *A*, *B* and *D* in the
word בְּרַת 31, 13.

(G) Omissions (IX, 3). An initial ו is omitted[1] by *C*
before לֹא 8, 21 but this alters the sense of the passage.
By *A* before הָא 20, 13 which makes this remarkable Hag.
passage run much more smoothly. By all MSS. before אִם
44, 27 where again an initial ו hardly seems necessary.

(H) Interchange of Prepositions and other Particles.
(IX, 5) *B* (incorrectly) בְּלִשְׁשִׁיחִין *A*, *C*, *D* and B. בְּלִישָׁנְהוֹן
10, 20. *C* (incorrectly) עַל אַרְעָא 44, 11. B., *A*, *B* and
D בְאַרְעָא. Hebrew אַרְצָהּ. In connection with this instance
and the following we may compare Nehemiah 3, 37 where
according to the occidentales (Palaestinenses) we should
read עַל and according to the orientales[2] (Babylonii) אֶל.
20, 2 *B* and *D* כָּלֵּהּ, *A*, *C* and B. בְּכָל 3. Hebrew
is אֶל to which לְ corresponds in Aramaic. 22, 12 MSS.

---

[1] Or 2374 sometimes omits ו where it is inserted in Baer's Edition
of the Aramaic portions of the Bible. Cf. יְדַ Daniel 2, 43, יִתְנַדְּבוּן
Daniel 3, 21, מְלַי Daniel 4, 9 in all of which the MS. omits the
initial ו. The Scribe however inserted this ו in מַלְכָּא Daniel 4, 13
in which case it is omitted in Baer's Edition.   [2] Vide Baer,
(l. c.), p. 125.   [3] "There is a tendency in Hebr. esp.
in S, K, Je, Ez, to use אֶל in the sense of עַל (and vice versa) sometimes אֶל being used quite exceptionally in a phrase or construction
which regularly and in acc. with analogy has עַל, sometimes the 2 preps.

בְּלֵילְיָא, B. לְלֵילְיָא. L. allows either reading here. 22, 18 לְמִדְבְּרָא which the MSS. have is a better reading than that given by B. who has בְּמַדְבְּרָא which appears to be a Hebraism, corresponding to the Hebrew בַּמִּדְבָּר. 31, 21. Unlike the Hebrew text which simply gives הַר, the Aramaic language requires a Preposition to point out the direction. A, B, D and B. give לְטוּרָא whilst C has בְּטוּרָא, one reading being as correct as the other. Either reading is again allowable in 37, 22 where B has בְּטוּרָא whilst A, C, D and B. give לְטוּרָא. Hebrew אֶל הָהוּר. 41, 55 A, D לְטוּרָא; B, C and B. עַל טוּרָא which appears more correct. The Hebrew text is לְהָרָם. 3, 12 B לֵהּ A, C, D and B. עִם. B's reading is inferior, although it gives sense. 3, 17 B הָא. The rest, more correctly אֲרֵי. The Hebrew is כִּי. 3, 23 B., A, C, D אַרְעָא, B אַרְעָא דָּא. The text being הָאֲרָדָה אֵת I prefer B's reading and the Path-egen also seems to expect B's reading. 4, 8 B and B. לְטַהֵשׁ, A and C לְטַהֵשׁ, D לְטַהֵשׁ לְטוּר. Adler in נֹגַהּ נְתִינָה justifies the reading of A and C; he says we never find the Verb קם construed with אֶל but with בְּ or עַל. B. and B's reading would then be a Hebraism; whilst D's reading is inferior, inasmuch as it indicates a slower movement than that shown by the Hebrew text. 6, 13 B., A, C, D עִם, B יָד. Hebrew is אֵת = with. The sense of B's reading is "from off the face of the earth" but this idea is not contained in the Hebrew אֵת and hence B's reading is again incorrect. 14, 7 B. אִהָא, C לֵהּ, A, B and D הָא. C's reading is incorrect; (as regards the difference of Gender, v. Pt. II, II, 7c). 15, 16 B., A, B, D הַלְכָא, C הָכָא. Hebrew is הַנֵּה. Both readings are correct; both are composed of the words הָא and כָא but הלכה has a liquid ל inserted. Cf.

---

interchanging apparently without discrimination in the same or parallel sentences. It is prob. that this interchange, at least in many cases, is not original but due to transcribers" Heb. and Eng. Lexicon of O. Test. by Brown, Briggs & Driver, Oxford 1892. s. v. אֵל) cf. also Jeremiah 27, 19.

Syriac ܩܕܡܘܗܝ. 18, 19 B (incorrectly) בְּמֵיהּ, B., A, C and D בְּמֵיהּ but, on the other hand, B's reading בְּמֵיהּ is preferable to that of the remaining MSS. and B. viz קָדָמוֹהִי 18, 29. The Hebrew is אֶלָיו. Perhaps קדמוהי was used to avoid the anthropomorphism "in His presence" and not "with Him". 19, 34 A (incorrectly) עִם, B., B, C, D עִם. Hebrew is אֵת = with. 24, 7 B עִל, A, C, D and B. לְ. Hebrew לְ. B's reading appears to be preferable since קם is usually construed with עַל in Aramaic. 20, 40 A, B and C קָדָמָךְ. D and B. קָמָךְ. This latter reading is the correct one, the text being אַתָּה, although the other reading may perhaps be justified. 27, 6 B בֵּהּ, A, C, D and B. בָּהּ. Although Landauer justifies the latter reading in his Massorah, still we must notice that the Hebrew את is here merely the sign of the Accusative, which would justify B's reading. 27, 37 B הָכָא A, C, D and B. כֵּן. Since it is rather time than place that is here indicated by אֵיפֹא, B's reading seems faulty. A כֵּן, B, C, D and B. כֵּן 28, 15. The Hebrew is אֲשֶׁר אִי and A gives the sense of this relative more clearly. B (incorrectly) הָכָא 31, 5, B., A, C, D אָן. Hebrew is פֹּה. B (incorrectly) כֵּן. Rest הָכָא 31, 37. The latter reading corresponds to the Hebrew פֹּה = here. B is again wrong in 31, 43 where he reads כִּי exactly as the Hebrew text, but the Aramaic idiom here requires a ד and hence the reading of B., A, C and D viz דִּילֵי is correct. B is again wrong in 35, 1 where he has לָךְ corresponding to the Hebrew אֵלֶיךָ. The other MSS. have לָךְ and גַּבָּא is usually construed with לְ.

The less emphatic Particles are the correct ones in 19, 38 viz דִּין (and not as B הָדֵין) and in 35, 17 and 20 דִּין (and not הָדֵין as A and C have). 37, 35 B (text) עַל. B (margin), A, C, D כֹּל. Hebrew is אֶל. Raši says that here אֶל = עַל which would justify B's original reading, but כֹּל is certainly more literal. 38, 12 B. has עֲנִית; all the MSS. read

---

[1] V. Note to 20, 2 above.

כל. The unknown author of the Pathšegen also reads as B. לוה is usually the Trg. for אל whilst the Preposition על is identical in both languages. Hence the text of the MSS. is superior here. 39, 7 B. and C בחיל, B בחיל, A and D קליח חיל. The Hebrew is אל. Although the MSS. readings may be defended still that of B. and C is here the best. So also Pathšegen. נקם is usually construed with ב. Cf. Trg. to Deut. 32, 4. 42, 28 C has היא הוא which is not such a good rendering of the Hebrew עין היה as the other MSS. and B. have, these give הוא בה. I do not know why B. has לכרך as the Trg. of לך in 43, 9. All four MSS. read לך. 43, 11 B., B (text), C and D have היא whilst A and B (margin) read הוא. The Hebrew text is איא to which word הוא usually corresponds, but in this particular verse איא is merely an emphatic particle. 43, 23. The Hebrew text being אלי the reading of the MSS. לדיך appears to be superior to that of B. which has לי. On the other hand B.'s reading is preferable in 45, 10 where he reads לכרך and the MSS. לי. The Hebrew is again אלי. 44, 4. In this verse we have another special use of the Hebrew word את, the sense of which is 'from' and hence the MSS. render מן. B. (incorrectly) ית. For a similar use of את cf. בצאת את העיר (Exodus 9, 29) where, however, all the MSS. have מן. 47, 10 B (incorrectly) לבלי, A, C, D and B. מן קדם. The Hebrew text is לבלתי.

(I) Hebraisms (VII, 19). Of actual Hebraisms C presents the most instances. I have previously remarked that this MS. does not differ so greatly from the Trg. text of B. as the other MSS. do. Yet B reads בדה בקר 27, 17. C has בחצי 27, 34 and 38 and בש 11, 29; 21. 3 whilst B reads the same word in 41, 45. B has בן (for בר) 21, 9. All the MSS. read אחרי 27, 9, when we should expect בתר as B. A has בצרים 41, 55 and 47, 15. C and D בה 4, 15. The rest read בן. C has קפדי 37, 18. It should be פרדי. All have חלחלה 35, 21 &c. B and D שבע 26, 33. B's Hebraism שה 38, 1 and that of all the MSS. היה 43, 6 have already been noticed above, when speaking of the variations in the use of the Particles.

(J) Variant readings (X). *A* and *D* הֽדְאִית (so also B.) 1, 11. *B* הֱוֵית. As a mere translation of the Hebrew words תַּדְשֵׁא הָאָרֶץ דֶּשֶׁא the version of *B* would suffice "Let the earth bring forth green". But as the Trg., in most cases, not only tries to translate the original but actually goes out of its way to obtain an identical form, the reading of *A*, *D* and B. seems superior.

2, 8 *A* וְיַשֵּׁי[1], *B* and *D* וְאַשְׁרִי. B. יַאֲשְׁרֵי. Pathšegen objects to *A*'s reading "ואשרי תרגם ולא ושוי" Nevertheless *A* gives a more literal rendering of the Hebrew יָשֶׂם than does the word וְאַשְׁרִי — which means "And he made to dwell". 2, 14 *A* חִדֶּקֶל, *B*, *D* and B. דִּגְלַת. *A* is probably a Hebraism, the Aramaic name of the Tigris being דִּגְלַת. Syriac ܕܶܩܠܰܬ. Assyrian Tiglat[2]. Arabic دِجْلَة. L. says the Hebrew form of the word has a prosthetic ח just as חֲבַצֶּלֶת from בצל. 2, 24 B., *A* and *D* have here בֵּית מֹשְׁבְּבֵי אֲבוֹתֵי אַמֵּיהּ but *B* ר׳ אֲבוּהִי דֶּרֶר אִמֵּהּ[3]. The latter reading being quite literal is superior to the former. The Hebrew text is אֶת אָבִיו וְאֶת אִמּוֹ. The other version has reference to a traditional translation of these words by the Rabbis Eliézer and Akiba[4]. 3, 1 B. עָרִים, MSS. חֹכִים. To understand the reading of the MSS., we may compare 27, 35 where בְּרָמָה is rendered בְּחָכְמָה[5] in the Trg.; but according to the Pathšegen חכים is only applied to men. The Syriac ܚܰܟܺܝܡܳܐ is also used for cunning. 3, 22 *B* (incorrectly) הֲנָה. The rest have הָוֵא. Heb. הַחַיִּים. 4, 3 B. and *D* קַדְבְּלָא, *A* אַקְרוּבָהּ, *B* תִּקְרָבָה, *C* גֻּדְחָא. Which is correct? The

---

[1] Samaritan וישוי. [2] Or Dignat, Tignat, Diqlat (?). Cf. also LXX. Τίγρις. [3] So Samaritan ית אמה וית אבוה. [4] V. Ber. Massorah p. 117 and Adler נדרש כל׳ to this verse. [5] According to Dalman Jewish Aramaic does not emply the root חכם in the simple signification of "to know", this use being confined to Galilean Aramaic. The corresponding Jewish Aramaic root is ידע (l. c. p. 38).

Hebrew is מִנְחָה[1]. L. and Path͏̆egen both give קִרְבָּנָא, and if the word מנחה here means 'offering' this is the only correct translation. But it must be borne in mind that the word can also mean a present (Arabic منح = to give) and this would justify both *A* and *C*'s reading. *B* is wrong. Luz. says the reading תקרובתא is bad, as this word is only used when speaking of persons making presents to each other and never in connection with God[2]. 4, 21 B. וְיָדַע, *A* דמנע, *B* הֲלֹה, *C* יְדַע, *D* הֲמִלֵּין. As if we have not already sufficient variations, Path͏̆egen wishes to read דְיָדַע or דְמָנְעִין. The Hebrew is הֲשַׁב. Path͏̆egen goes on to say that the reading דמנע is a mistake, and I can find no sense in B., *D*, *B* or *C*, the readings of the two last-mentioned MSS. not being even correct Aramaic forms (but cf. Berliner p. 128 who justifies his reading). Yet *D*'s reading seems to be the original one since *A* had this word in the text, but it was afterwards erased and דמנע placed on the margin in its place. Probably the whole phrase דמנע על פם נבלא should be deleted from the Trg. text as superfluous. For similar double translations cf. 3, 21; 4, 21; 24, 21; 30, 8; 40, 10; 49, 4 and 49, 8 in the latter we have even a treble rendering.

5, 3 B. דְדָבֵיהּ לֵיהּ, *A*, *C*, *D* הַדְבֵי ליה, *B* בְּצַלְמֵהּ. The Hebrew is כְּצַלְמוֹ and hence *B*'s reading is the most literal. Of course the other readings give the sense of the Hebrew passage. Path͏̆egen reads as *A*, *C*, *D*. 5, 24 B. has אֲמִית הֲוֵה, *A* has לָא אֲמִית הֲוֵה whilst *B*, *C*, *D* insert לא on the margin. This great difference probably has its origin in some Hag. point. Luz. in Philoxenos[3] remarks "he (Enoch) is still living for God did not kill him". In Tosafoth to Yebamoth 166 s. v. פשום we read of a difference among Hagadoth one tradition being that Enoch died whilst another records that

---

[1] It is noteworthy that a similar variant reading occurs in the different Editions of the Samaritan Targum, the Editions of Brull and Uhlemann both giving מנחתה whilst that of Petermann reads מנחה.

[2] Philoxenos p. 31.   [3] p. 32.

he entered Paradise whilst still alive[1]. The Trg. text is there quoted without וְלֹא and without troubling ourselves about the different traditions, we can see by the original Hebrew text that לֹא is out of place here, but we can understand and notice how it crept into the text.

9, 2 *A* בְּרָא, B., *B, C, D* אָרְעָא which is of course the correct Trg. of הָאָרֶץ. *A* means 'wild beasts' which gives sense but is not the correct translation of the Hebrew. 10, 30 B. בְּתְחוֹן, *B, C, D* בְּלְבַבְחוֹן, *A* בְּנֵיהוֹן מוֹת! *A*'s reading is an absurdity[2]. 11, 3 B., *A, C, D* כַּהֲבָה[3], *B* לְאַחֲוָה. Hebrew רֵחָהּ. The readings are here equally good. 11, 3 *B* וְיִשְׁצֵינוּן, B., *A, C, D* וְיִשְׁצֵרוּנוּן. Hebrew וְיֵיבְשָׁה. B. is incorrect since יקד is (according to L.) Intransitive. Similarly Luz. says in his גר אחב[4] that יקד is only used for entirely consuming and not for merely drying. Pathšegen also justifies the reading וְנֵשִׁיצֵינוּן. 11, 6 *C* הַשִּׁיצֵא[1] B., *A, B, D* הֶחֱרִבֵי. *C* has simply confused the end of the verse with the first וְשֵׁיצֵיאוּ. 11, 31 B., *B* and *C* וּדְבַר, *A, D* וּנְסִיב. The first-mentioned reading is more correct[5]. There are two Aramaic Verbs corresponding to the Hebrew root לקח (1) דבר when speaking of to lead from one place to another (2) נסב simply to take, or with אִתְּתָא = to marry. But some confusion is noticeable in the use of these two Aramaic roots. B. has דְבַר 14, 21 but all the MSS. here נסב[6]. L. here again reads דבר. Again in 24, 67 *B* has וּדְבַר, *A, C, D* and B. וּנְסִיב[7]. Here it means to marry, hence *B* is wrong. Finally in 30, 9 *B* דְבַשָּׁא[8], B., *A, C, D* דַבְרָהּ[1] in which case *B* is again incorrect. 13, 9 B. and *C* כַּלְפֵּי אָנָא, *A, B, C* (margin) and *D* אָזְלֵינַן. Hebrew וְנַאַשְׂרָבָה. The Trg. here renders

---

1) Cf. Bezold's "Schatzhöhle" Leipzig 1888, II, p. VI, also Qoran, Sura 19, 57 and 58 where Edris is identified by Abulfeda with Enoch (Cf. Abulfedae Historia Anteislamica: Ed. Fleischer, Leipzig 1831, p. 13).
2 But מוֹחֵבֵיהֹן (in one word) = "their seats" and would therefore be correct.   3 Likewise the Samaritan has לֶהֱבָה.   4 l. c. p. 33.
5 Although the Samaritan has נסב, cf. also Singer l. c. p. 21.
6 Samaritan נסב.   7 Samaritan נסב.   8 Samaritan דברה.

the Hebrew text ad sensum. The manuscript reading comes nearer to the Hebrew in form, whilst B. and C (text) make the verse run more smoothly in Aramaic. L. appears to read as B. since he gives no verbal root יבז in his Dictionary. 15, 11 B., *B* (text), *D* אֲהָרֵב, *C* אֲהָרֵב, *A*, *B* (margin) הֲרֵאָם. The difference in vocalization has already been treated of above. L. reads as *A* and *B* (margin) "he drove them away". On the other hand Luz.[1] takes the reading ואהרם as a marginal gloss, which, although incorrect, subsequently crept into the text. Pathšegen[2] says the traditional Trg. is ואתיב and this reading appears preferable, although so great an authority as L. reads otherwise. 15, 18 B. and *C* הֲחֵיב[3] *A*, *B*, *D* אֲרִין. Hebrew יַחֲת. B.'s reading is preferable, but the sense of the passage is Future, and therefore the manuscript reading, though inferior, may perhaps be justified. As regards the different roots used, L. solves our difficulty by telling us that the only parts of נחת in use in Aramaic are the Future and Infinitive. 17, 2 B., *A*, *C*, *D* בֵּין מֵימְרֵי, *B* בֵינִי[4]. Hebrew בֵּינִי. Pathšegen supports the former version. This expression is another instance of the Targumist's constant endeavour to avoid anthropomorphic expressions; whilst *B* translates literally. The suffix of the 1st Person Singular is wanting in this word and in אֲבָא according to L.[5] Hence בֵּיתִי = בֵּיתָא. 18, 21 B. and *C* (text) have אִם אָף הָכְדֵין לֹא אֲכַלָּא, *A*, *B*, *C* (margin) and *D* read אִם לֹא הָכְדֵין אָף הָכְדֵין לֹא אֲכַלָּא. The Hebrew text is simply וְאִם לֹא אֵדָעָה. All the commentators have remarks to make on this peculiarly difficult passage. Luz., Pathšegen and Adler all justify B.'s Text "I will (make an end with you, come to terms with

---

[1] l. c. p. 35. [2] To this verse. [3] Samaritan יחתו. [4] Samaritan ביני. [5] Dalman likewise mentions the avoidance of this suffix in his grammar p. 162 "Die Form des Suff. der 1 Pers. Sing. nach vokal. Auslaut sollte wohl i sein. Sie wird aber geflissentlich vermieden und bei אָב (und אָם) durch die det. Form ersetzt". But he places בַּיִת under those words in which the diphthong ai became weakened to a. Thus בַּיִת = בֵּיתִי cf. also עֵינַי = עֵינָי &c.

you) forgive you, if you repent but if not, I shall punish you". The corrected (MS.) reading runs "I shall (make an end with you) destroy you, if you do not repent, but if you repent, I shall not punish you." Both readings, are, however, very obscure and it is very doubtful whether either is correct. 19, 33 B., *B* and *C* בֹּלָּה, *A* and *D* הִקְמָה. The text is וַתֵּבֹא. *A* and *D* are both wrong, they probably wrote הִקְמָה through confusion with verse 35 of which the Hebrew is וַהֲקִמֹ. 19, 33 and 35 *C* (margin) בִשְׁבֹה וּבְקִלְמֹה¹. B., *A*, *B*, *C* (text) and *D* בִמְשְׁבֹה בִמְקִלְמֹה, *C*'s marginal (corrected?) readings merely appear to be Hebraisms.

21, 33 *C* אִי־לָלֹא, B., *A*, *B* and *D* אִבָּלֹא. The Hebrew original is אֲשֶׁל. L. reads as B. The reading אִי־לָלֹא is probably a marginal note which crept into the text, and in some MSS. supplanted the more correct reading. In *A* a later hand has already inserted אילנא on the margin. 22, 12 *B* (text) שָׁבַקְתָּא, B., *A*, *B* (margin), *C*, *D* אֲבָלְתָּא² which is undoubtedly the proper text; so L. שבקת = "Thou hast forsaken" and not "thou hast withheld" which the Hebrew חָשַׂכְתָּ means. 22, 18 *B* is again incorrect in this verse in which we find בְּדִילָךְ written instead of בְּדִיל דַּל which is the correct Trg. of בְּעֲבוּרְךָ. 23, 6 B. and *C* בְּלִי, *B* בַּלִּי, *A*, *D* יְמֵי³. The only noticeable difference between *C* and *B* is the fact that *C* (as usual) has a form exactly like that of B. whilst *B* preserves the punctuation of the Superlinear system more distinctly. The Hebrew is כָּלָה. Both Berliner and Landauer in their Massorahs give this word as an instance of קרא ותרגום. Similarly, the author of the Path̄egen. According to these authorities, the first-mentioned reading is the correct one. But it has already been noticed that our MSS. do not follow these Massoretic rules of קרא ותרגום. At the same time ימי conveys the sense of the original and both Raši⁴ and Ibn Ezra explain יכלה = ימי. 24, 10 *B*

---

¹ Likewise the Samaritan has בששבה יבקימה. ² Samaritan מִיעָה.
³ Samaritan ימיי. ⁴ a. l.

-בֵּ֫. B., A, C and D כֹּלָ which is the same word as that given in the Hebrew text, and hence, perhaps, a Hebraism. 24, 19 B (incorrectly) כְּלִבְלָי, A, B (margin), C, D and B. לְבְלֵישִׁי. 24, 21 B., A, D בֵּה שָׁהֵי, B בֵּה שָׁהֵי, C בֵּה שָׁהֵי. Pathšegen accepts the latter reading, but L. writes as B. and as early as Rashi's time the reading of C was already pointed out as incorrect. The Hebrew text is בָּאֲרָה כָּה. Berliner in his Massorah places שָׁהֵי בָה as a Suraan reading whilst שָׁהֵי וּבָה falls under the head of the Nehardean readings. 24, 38 B (text) וּלְבִלְדִּי בָּאֵישׁ-שָׁ B (margin) and the remaining texts לְבֵיתָה אֲבָא וּלְזַרְעִיתִי. Since the corresponding Hebrew is אֶל בֵּית אָבִי יָאֶל מִשְׁפַּחְתִּי the last-mentioned text is more literal and hence, perhaps, preferable[1]. 24, 44 B. אִשְׁתֵּי, A and B (margin) אַבְלִי, B (text) אַשְׁקִי, C אַבְלִי, D אַבְלִי. The Hebrew is אֶשְׁאָב "I shall draw". Although none of the readings here mentioned give us a literal translation of the Hebrew still אַשְׁקִי is undoubtedly incorrect. (for the differences of vocalization see above).

24, 59 B. and C גַּבְרִיחֵי, B and D בְּחֵיל, A גְּבוּרְהָא. A appears to have taken the Hebrew אֲנָשָׁיו in the sense of 'warriors' but there is nothing in the context which admits of such an interpretation. The vowel-changes have already been noticed. 24, 62. The Hebrew text runs וְיִצְחָק בָּא מִבֹּא בְּאֵר of which the Targum is—according to B כַּד עַל מִבְלַל לְמֵיתִי בְּבֵירָא whilst the other versions give וְיִצְחָק עַל כַּד מִתְיְהִיב לֵהּ בֵּירָא. We can reject both these versions and follow that given by Nachmanides[2] אָתָא מִבְּחִיתֵיהּ which is more literal. 25, 6 B., C and D have לִבְנֵי פִּילַגְשָׁיָא דִּי לְאַבְרָהָם, A בְּנֵי לָחֱנָתָא whilst B has לִבְנֵי לָחֱנָתָא דִּי לְאַבְרָהָם. The Hebrew text is קֵדְמָה אֶל אֶרֶץ קֶדֶם. A is the best and most literal translation and is supported by the authority of L. and Pathšegen. 25, 25 B., B, C בְּגֵז, A בְּגַלִין, D בְּגֵז. The Hebrew text is אַדֶּרֶת. L. explains all these words to be of similar signification and

---

[1] Cf. LXX 'Αλλ' εἰς τὸν οἶκον τοῦ πατρός μου πορεύσῃ καὶ εἰς τὴν φυλήν μου. [2] To this verse q. v.

all mean 'cloak' or 'mantle'. B.'s reading being derived from
κυκλάς sc. ἐσθής that of *A* from the Persian كلم and that
of *D* from the Greek χλαῖνα. Pathšegen also reads בכלן
and explains that a כ comparationis is omitted because the
word is used adjectively and not substantively. 26, 14 *C*
(margin) פבלהא, *C* (text) and remainder שבהלה just as the
Hebrew. This instance is also mentioned in Berliner's
Massorah under קרא ותרגום. Pathšegen also gives כבודה. It
is, however, remarkable that in the quotation of this verse
by Theodorus Mopsuestenus[1], who lived at the beginning of
the 5th century, he uses the word ܡܥܦܪܐ, although the
Pešitta which he usually quotes has here ܟܚܕܬܐ. Mopsuestenus
is, however, by no means exact in his quotations from the
Pešitta, his rendering of Biblical passages frequently differs
both from Trg. and Pesitta. 26, 18 *C* (text) דקרי. *C* (margin),
A, *B*, *D* and B. קָדֵי דַהֲוָה. Hebrew is קָרָא for which we
might expect the Trg. to be דקרא. 27, 3 *B* after omitting
קָשְׁתֶּךָ in its text, gives the incorrect marginal reading ורומחך.
27, 31 B. יַאֲצֵיל, *B* and *D* דְאֵצִיל, *C* וְאָצֵיל, *A* וְאַיְתִי. Of these
readings only that of *C* is incorrect. Although the Tar-
gumic form usually corresponding with the Hiphil of בוא in
Hebrew is the Aphel of ללל, still we also occasionally find
the Aphel of אתא thus employed. (Cf. 27, 7). 27, 34 *B*
אָנֹא[2]. The rest have לִי. Hebrew is אָנִי. *B* imitates the
peculiar construction of the Hebrew original; but לִי is the
correct Trg. Luz.[3] remarks "Those who would read אנא
forget that it is not the object of the Targumist to retain
the Hebrew obscurities, but rather to clear them up". 29, 8
B. and *C* יִנְהֲדרוּן, *A*, *D* וְיִנְהֲדרוּן, *B* יִהְנַהֲדרִין. The Hebrew is
יְגֵלְלוּ. L. permits either reading, taking the reading of *A* and
D as a "Gafel" form of נדר. Raši also reads the word with
a prosthetic ג. *B* has a mistake in the Gender. 30, 6 *B*
has קביל צללי די איש לבעותי ר"ה צללין. B., *A*, *C* and *D* simply

---

[1] Edit. Sachau, Leipzig 1879 (page ܣܡ).   [2] Samaritan אנכ.
[3] l. c. p. 41.

read אָבֵ֤ל כָּבֵ֣יל בְּלִילָ֑ה which corresponds literally to the Hebrew יַ֖עַב שָׂמֵ֥חַ בְּקוֹלִֽי. The first part of B's rendering is perhaps a marginal gloss which was afterwards inserted in the text by an ignorant scribe. 30, 15 B., D and B (margin) לֹהּ, A and B (text) לֹאָהּ[1]. C is missing. Since the Hebrew text reads לֹהּ, the reading לֹאָהּ although giving the sense of the passage appears to be incorrect. 31, 2 B., A and C (text) לְחֶהֵן[2], C (margin), לְהֵיהּ, B בְּלִיהֵן, D הִיהֵן. The Hebrew is אָרֵי. The forms given by B and D are incorrect. As the suffix refers to אב and not to בן C's marginal correction is worthless. But לִיהֵי would be a more correct Aramaic form. 31, 13 C (incorrectly) אַרְעָא הָדֵין. The other MSS. read אַרְעָא הָדָא which corresponds to the Hebrew הָאָ֣רֶץ הַזֹּ֑את. 31, 16. In this verse B's reading הַשִׁירוּב appears to be preferable to the text given by B., A, C and D which give הַאֲשֵׁרוּב "who separated". The Hebrew text is אֲשֶׁ֣ר הִצִּ֔יל. 31, 21 B אֲהָלְ הֵלֵהּ. The rest have יָה פְּרֵהּ. Neither are literal since the Hebrew is simply הַיָּה. Pathsegen similar to B., A, C and D. It is difficult to say which reading is preferable, but perhaps B is, since it preserves the word of the Hebrew text נֵהר. 31, 29 C (text) אַלְבָּ֣א לְבִיל, C (margin) and the others מִלְבָּלְבָּא[3]. The Hebrew being מִדַּבֵּר the latter reading is correct. C (text) gives the sense of the original but is not literal. 34, 7 B. וְאֵיתְנַסִּיאַ, A, B, D וְאִצְטָעֲרוּ, C וְאִצְטַעֲרוּ. The meaning of the former reading is "And the men were tried" which gives no sense here. On the other hand the reading of C—which is also given by L.— gives us the correct sense "And the men were grieved" which exactly corresponds to the Hebrew וַיִּתְעַצְּב֣וּ. In this verse then I think we should reject the reading given by B. in favour of that shown by C. 34, 7 B (text) אָ֣ישׁ, B (margin) and the rest גַּבְרָא[4]. Hebrew נַ֥עַר. Which is the better reading? In verse 27 of this chapter all render אִ֖ישׁ by גַּבְרָא so that

---

[1] LXX also Λεια.   [2] Samaritan לְהֵהֵן.   [3] Samaritan מְלַלְלָא.
[4] Samaritan עלי.

perhaps this reading should be preferred. But there are many passages in the Trg. in which the Aramaic Verbal Root which corresponds to the Hebrew בוא is אתא. We may perhaps then accept either of the above-mentioned readings. 35, 3 B בְּעִדָּן עָקְתִי. The rest have בְּיוֹמָא דְעָקְתִי [1] which is the correct Trg. of the Hebrew בְּיוֹם צָרָתִי. It is true that B gives us the exact sense of the original, but yet the reading is faulty. 35, 8 B מִתְּחִית. Rest have מִלְרַע [2]. Hebrew מִתָּחַת. As an instance of the close connection between these two Aramaic words compare מלרע לרקיעא 1, 7 and again מתחות שמיא 1, 9. The words are really synonyms but Path*egen [3] tries to make a distinction between them by saying that one refers to a greater depth than the other and that a fine distinction does exist in the use of the two words may be seen by comparing the Heb. of 1, 7 and 1, 9. 1, 7 has לתחת whilst 1, 9 has only תחת, the Trg. for 1, 7 being מלרע ל and for 1, 9 מתחות. As the ל is also used here מלרע seems preferable. 35, 18 D (incorrectly) בְּעִדָּן. The other MSS. and B. read בְּמִפָּק which is the correct Trg. of the Hebrew בְּצֵאת. 36, 35 B., C and D בְּחַקְלֵי מוֹאָב, A בְּחַקְלָא דְמוֹאָב, B בַּאֲלֵי מוֹאָב. The original has בִּשְׂדֵה מוֹאָב of which A gives the most literal Aramaic. B is decidedly incorrect. 37, 2 A דִבְחוֹן. The other MSS. and B. read טִיבְחוֹן. Authorities differ which of these readings we should prefer. Berliner in his Massorah[4] remarks "Many copies have the incorrect reading דבהון which imitates the word given in the Hebrew text; the Aramaic word טיב first bore the meaning of calumniating when joined with בישא". Similarly Luz.[5] after citing many passages in which the Hebrew דיבה = the Aramaic טיב adds that the reading דיבה is nothing more nor less than a mistake. On the other hand L.[6] remarks; "Since our root (טיב) hardly ever occurs in the Babylonian Trg. in this signification (viz. that of calumniation) therefore the reading

[1] Samaritan ביום עקתי.   [2] Samaritan מלרע.   [3] To this verse.
[4] p. 78.   [5] Philoxenos p. 43.   [6] s. v.

דּבָהֹן is superior." We may therefore accept *A*'s reading as the correct one. 37, 23 *B* (margin) בְּלֹ¹, *B* (text), *A*, *C*, *D* and B. אָבָא. Hebrew בָּא (see above 34, 7). 37, 35 *B* (text) בְּד חֹזִין, *D* and *B* (margin) דּ אֲבִידָלָא, B., *A* and *C* דּ אָבִיד. L. although mentioning the latter reading gives as correct the text given by *D* and *B* (margin). But how is the version of *B* (text) to be explained? It appears to be an allusion to the Jewish doctrine of the Immortality of the soul, but is, of course, an interpolation. The Hebrew original is simply אָבָל. 37, 2 B. בְּכִנְעָן², *A*, *D* הָלֹ, *B* אָבְנֹ, *C* בְּכִנָן. The Hebrew has כִּנְעַן. L. and Pathsegen both give the correct reading as בִּכְנַעֲנָאֵי although L. also mentions the other rendering. But before we are able to give an opinion which reading is preferable, it is necessary to be quite clear about the signification of the Hebrew original and here the authorities differ. Raši, R. Samuel b. Meir, Nachmanides, Gersonides and Mendelssohn render "merchant" whilst the Revised English Version, Ibn Ezra, the LXX and Pešitta translate "Canaanite". Adler aptly remarks in his נתיבה בגד³ that the rendering "merchant" is given to spare Judah's honour, he also quotes Talmud and Midraš in support of this translation. But after all I think the most correct reading is that given by L. which is literal. 38, 17 B. אֲשַׁלַּח, *A*, *C* and *D* אֲשַׁדֵּר, *B* אשׁלח⁴. Hebrew אֲשַׁלָּה. The readings given by B. and *B* are equally good, since the Afel of שלח is merely a little stronger than the Peal, but the reading אֲשַׁדֵּר is wrong according to L. who quotes Levita to prove that the root שדר only occurs in 38, 20 and 23 where, according to the author of the Pathsegen, it has the signification of 'giving' merely, and not as here giving with the idea of repayment *i. e.* as a loan. 41, 5 *A* בְּלִבֵּן. The other MSS. have בְּלִבֵּהּ which is the correct reading, according to L., although בְּלִבֵּן has precisely the same meaning as בְּלִבֵּהּ. 41, 30

---

¹ Samaritan אֲבָל.   ² Samaritan בִּכְנַעֲנָאֵי   ³ To this verse.
⁴ Samaritan אשׁלה.

B (text) הֲוָה אֲ־לָא, B (margin), A, C, D and B. בָּלָא דְאַרְעָא.
One would only expect אֲ־לָא תהי[1] but as Adler points out in
his גרי תהינה: a. l. the root כלה is more applicable to the
ruin of the inhabitants of a country than to the ruin of the
country itself. We must therefore either assume that both
versions are faulty or that both are equally good. 42, 10
A (incorrectly) חֵי, B. אֱהִי. B, C and D אֵי. The Hebrew
is בָּאוּ. 42, 38 A בְּבִישְׁתָא. B, C, D בְּדִוְנָא. The Hebrew
is בְּיָגוֹן. A gives the correct sense but is an inferior reading.
L. also has בדוונא. On the other hand B is incorrect in
giving בְּדִוְנָא as the Trg. for the Hebrew בְּרָעָה in 44, 29.
The other MSS. and B. here give בְּבִישְׁתָא which is correct.
43, 5 B (text) אָחְתָּה דְלָא כְסִילָא, B (margin) and the rest
אָח לָא. B's mistake is one of homoioteleuton. cf. v. 3.
43, 18 A (incorrectly) דְאִתְחַבַּל. The others have דְאָתָהּ which
is the correct Trg. of חָשַׁב. 44, 2 A דְבִנְיָמִן, rest דוּשִׁילָא. Hebrew
הַקָּטוֹן hence A is wrong although, of course, the verse refers
to Benjamin. 44, 14 B כָּל אֶחָיו, rest have קְדָמוֹהִי, The
Hebrew is לְפָנָיו and hence B (which would be the Trg. of
כָּל פְּנֵיהֶם) is a mistake. 48, 19 A יִפְקוּן בְּנֵי בְּעַבְדַּיָא דְשָׁלְטִין וּמַלְכִין.
B, C and D give וּבְנוֹהִי יְהוֹן שָׁלְטִין בְּעַמְמַיָּא. So B. who employs
שָׁלְטִין instead of מַלְכִין. The Hebrew original is וְזַרְעוֹ
יִהְיֶה בִּמְלֹא־הַגּוֹיִם. Both renderings are equally free and hence
hardly satisfactory, although we must bear in mind that in
some of the poetical and prophetical passages of the Pentateuch, O. doubtless allowed himself great freedom in giving
the sense of the original, besides which our texts of the
Trg. are frequently hopelessly corrupt. Of the two renderings
here given A's is historically inaccurate, as the great Hebrew
kings who ruled over other nations sprang from the tribe
of Judah and not from that of Ephraim. But the tribe
of Ephraim was the most powerful of the kingdom of Israel
and hence the other rendering is at least historically true.
The Hebrew text is very obscure, but whatever it does

[1] As the Samaritan Trg. gives.

mean is not represented by either of the Targumic versions here quoted. A "fullness of nations" probably means "exceedingly numerous". 48, 22 B. and C (text) בְּכוּפְרֵי בִּרְכָתָא, C (margin), A, B and D בְּגוֹ בְּנֵי בְּעֵילְמָא which is a Hag. rendering. V. Raši and Adler in his יד בגו on this verse. The Targumist strives to soften the apparent harshness of Jacob's language. B.'s reading is quite literal. 49, 27 B., B, C קְרֹיבָא, A עֲשִׂירָא, D קְרֵיבָא. Although the Hebrew original is amplified in this verse to such an extent that it becomes all but unrecognisable in the Aramaic translation, still of the renderings here given the first mentioned is the only one that gives the correct Aramaic word and therefore the only reading we can here adopt.

This is a complete list of the Variae lectiones and it may be seen by a perusal of these together with the vowel changes and grammatical irregularities which we have already noticed how very far we are from having a correct critical text of the Trg. Undoubtedly B.'s edition is a vast improvement upon the texts which preceded his, but we have seen how very often it may be improved upon. I am afraid it is too much for us to expect the Trg. text to be perfectly accurate since many later scribes have tampered with the text to such an extent that in many places we cannot recognise the Hebrew original at all in the Targumic translation. But what we may reasonably hope for is a gradual improvement until we shall have obtained a text which is as critical as we can possibly expect under the many disadvantageous conditions which surround the editing of such a text. As a first step in this direction I now give a few specimen chapters of the Trg. of O. with Superlinear vocalization, which, besides showing an improvement in language probably represents the original Palestinian Version.

III.

In the following chapters I have followed the MS. *D* which has already been noticed to give the best and clearest text. Occasionally I have inserted a reading which appears to be more correct in the foot-notes. My reasons for doing so may be found explained in the body of this work.

I also give the readings which are given by the Editio Bomberg (Venice, 1517) the text of which varies very considerably from the text of B.'s Edition. I have inserted every word in regard to which this Edition differs from that of B., although the reading may coincide with that of the MSS. The MSS. *C* and *D* invariably write the Tetragrammaton thus יְיָ whilst the Editio Bomberg writes ייי. *A* ייָ and *B* יְיָ [1]. The dot over the Śin is not written, Sin is written thus שׂ but is usually replaced by ס. The word קֳדָם is usually abbreviated in the MSS., which simply write קְ. In such cases the missing letters have been added in brackets. Numerous emendations appear to be necessary in the consonantal text, which should be purged from its numerous superfluous elements, but such corrections should be postponed until we have attained a more accurate vocalization [2].

Different chapters to those given by Merx in his "Chrestomathia Targumica" have purposely been chosen.

---

[1] Cf. Part I, Cp. II, 2. [2] Merx considers it necessary to apply both systems of vocalization to arrive at a correct and critical vocalized text, but it has been shown that this is possible by means of the Superlinear vocalization alone (cf. Merx "Bemerkungen", p. 188).

CHAPTER XVII.

(1) אֲהָה אַבְרָם בַּר תִּשְׁעִין וּתְשַׁע שְׁנִין אִתְגְּלִי יְיָ לְאַבְרָם
וַאֲמַר לֵיהּ אֲנָא אֵל שַׁדַּי פְּלַח קֳדָמַי וֶהֱוֵי שְׁלִים

(2) וְאֶתֵּן קְיָמִי בֵּין מֵימְרִי וּבֵינָךְ וְאַסְגֵּי יָתָךְ לַחְדָּא לַחְדָּא

(3) וּנְפַל אַבְרָם עַל אַפּוֹהִי וּמַלִּיל עִמֵּיהּ יְיָ לְמֵימָר

(4) אֲנָא הָא גְזַר קְיָמִי עִמָּךְ וּתְהֵי לְאַב סַגִּי עַמְמִין

(5) וְלָא יִתְקְרֵי עוֹד יָת שְׁמָךְ אַבְרָם וִיהֵי שְׁמָךְ אַבְרָהָם אֲרֵי
לְאַב סַגִּי עַמְמִין יְהַבְתָּךְ

(6) וְאַפֵּישׁ יָתָךְ לַחְדָּא לַחְדָּא וְאֶתְּנִנָּךְ לְכִנְשָׁן וּמַלְכִין
דְּשַׁלְטִין בְּעַמְמַיָּא מִנָּךְ יִפְּקוּן

(7) וַאֲקִים יָת קְיָמִי בֵּין מֵימְרִי וּבֵינָךְ וּבֵין בְּנָךְ בַּתְרָךְ
לְדָרֵיהוֹן לִקְיָם עָלַם לְמֶהֱוֵי לָךְ לֶאֱלָהּ וְלִבְנָךְ בַּתְרָךְ

(8) וְאֶתֵּן לָךְ וְלִבְנָךְ בַּתְרָךְ יָת אֲרַע תּוֹתָבוּתָךְ יָת כָּל אַרְעָא
דִכְנַעַן לְאַחְסָנַת עָלַם וֶאֱהֵי לְהוֹן לֶאֱלָהּ

(9) וַאֲמַר יְיָ לְאַבְרָהָם וְאַתְּ יָת קְיָמִי תִטַּר אַתְּ וּבְנָךְ בַּתְרָךְ
לְדָרֵיהוֹן

(10) דֵּין קְיָמִי דְּתִטְּרוּן בֵּין מֵימְרִי וּבֵינֵיכוֹן וּבֵין בְּנָךְ
בַּתְרָךְ מִגְזַר לְכוֹן כָּל דְּכוּרָא

(11) וְתִגְזְרוּן יָת בִּסְרָא דְעׇרְלַתְכוֹן וִיהֵי לְאָת קְיָם בֵּין
מֵימְרִי וּבֵינֵיכוֹן

a Edit. Bom. יְהִי. *b* Bom. יָאתֵן, *C* אֶתֵּן. *c* *B* אֶלָּא instead of בֵּין מֵימְרַי. *d* *B* לַחְדָא. *e* Bom. omits. *f* *C* קְדָמִי. *g* Bom. וִיהִי. *h* Bom. and *A* סָגֵי. *i* Bom. and *A* סְגִי, *B* אָג. *k* Bom. יְהַבְתָּךְ. *l* Bom. יָאפֵשׁ. *m* *C* אַתְּנִנָךְ. *n* Bom. בְּנִישִׁין. *o* Bom. דְּשַׁלְטִין. *p* Bom. יָקִים. The best form would be אָקִם. *q* Bom. לְבָחֲיֵי. *r* Bom. לֶאֱלָהָא, *B* לָאֱלָה. *s* Bom. יָאתֵן, *C* אֵתֵין. *t* Bom. כְּלָהּ. *u* Bom. אַתְיֵי, *C* אַחְיֵי. *x* Bom. יְאָמַר. *y* Bom. דָא. *z* Bom. תּוֹרֵיךְ. *aa* Bom. לְמִגְזַר, *C* לְמִגְזָר. *bb* Bom. וִיהֵי, *C* אִתְחֵי.

(12) וּבַר תַּמְנֵא יוֹמִין יִגְזַר לְכוֹן כָּל דְכוּרָא לְדָרֵיכוֹן יְלִיד
בֵּיתָא וּזְבִין בְּכַסְפָּא מִכֹּל בַּר עַמְמִין דְלָא מִבְּנָךְ הוּא
(13) מִגְזַר יִגְזַר יְלִיד[a] בֵּיתָךְ וּזְבִין[b] בְּכַסְפָּךְ[c] וִיהֵי[d] קְיָמִי
בְּבִסְרְכוֹן[e] לִקְיָם[f] עָלַם[g]
(14) וְעָרֵל דְכוּרָא דְלָא יִגְזַר יָת בְּסַר דְעָרְלָתֵיהּ[h] וְיִשְׁתֵּיצֵי
אֱנָשָׁא[i] הַהוּא מֵעַמֵּיהּ יָת קְיָמִי[k] אַשְׁנִי[l]
(15) וַאֲמַר יְיָ לְאַבְרָהָם שָׂרַי אִתְּתָךְ לָא תִקְרֵי יָת שְׁמַהּ[m] שָׂרָי
אֲרֵי שָׂרָה שְׁמַהּ
(16) וֶאֱבָרֵיךְ[n] יָתַהּ[o] וְאַף אִתֵּין[p] מִנַּהּ[q] לָךְ בַּר וֶאֱבָרֲכִנַהּ[r]
וּתְהֵי[s] לְעַמְמִין[t] וּמַלְכִין[u] דִשַׁלְטִין בְּעַמְמַיָא מִנַּהּ יְהוֹן
(17) וּנְפַל אַבְרָהָם עַל אַפּוֹהִי וַחֲדִי[x] וַאֲמַר בְּלִבֵּיהּ הֲלִבַר
מְאָה שְׁנִין יְהֵי[y] וְלַד[z] וְאִם שָׂרָה הֲבַת תִּשְׁעִין שְׁנִין תֵּלִיד[aa]
(18) וַאֲמַר אַבְרָהָם קֳ(דָם) יְיָ לְוַי[bb] דְיִשְׁמָעֵאל[cc] וְיִתְקַיָם[dd]
קֳדָמָךְ[ee]
(19) וַאֲמַר[ff] יְיָ בְּקוּשְׁטָא שָׂרָה אִתְּתָךְ תְּלִיד לָךְ בַּר וְתִקְרֵי יָת
שְׁמֵיהּ יִצְחָק וַאֲקִים[gg] יָת קְיָמִי[hh] עִמֵּיהּ לִקְיָם עָלַם[ii] לִבְנוֹהִי בַּתְרוֹהִי
(20) וְעַל יִשְׁמָעֵאל קַבֵּילִית צְלוֹתָךְ הָא בָּרֵיכִית יָתֵיהּ
וְאַפִּישִׁית[kk] יָתֵיהּ וְאַסְגֵיתִי[ll] יָתֵיהּ לַחֲדָא תְּרֵי[mm] עֲסַר רַבְרְבֵי
יוֹלִיד וְאֶתְּנִנֵיהּ[nn] לְעַם סַגִי

a A יְלִיד. *b* A וּזְבִינֵי. *c* B, C בְּכַסְפָּא, A בְּכַסְפָּא. *d* Bom. וִיהֵי. *e* Bom. בְּבִסְרְכוֹן, B בְּבִשְׂרְכוֹן. *f* Bom. לְקְיָם. *g* Bom. עֲלַם. *h* Bom. דְעָרְלָתֵיהּ. *i* Bom. אֱנָשָׁא. *k* B קְדָמַי. *l* Bom. אַשְׁנִי. *m* Bom. שְׁמַהּ. *n* Bom. יָאֲבָרֵךְ. *o* Bom. יָתַהּ. *p* Bom. אֶתֵּן, B אִתֵּין and omits אַף. *q* Bom. מִנַּהּ. The 3rd Sin. Fem. Suffix is always punctuated with Q. in this Edition, so this variation will not be noticed again. *r* Bom. וַאֲבָרְכִנַהּ. *s* Bom. וּתְהֵי. *t* Bom. לְעַמְמִין. *u* Bom. וּמַלְכִין. *x* Bom. וַחֲדִי. *y* Bom. יְהֵי. *z* Bom. וְלַד. *aa* B תֵּלִיד. *bb* לְוַי is a more correct form. *cc* A, B יִשְׁמָעֵאל. *dd* Bom. וְיִתְקַיָם. *ee* Bom. קֳדָמָךְ. *ff* Bom. וַאֲמַר. *gg* Bom. וַאֲקִים. *hh* C קְיָמִי. *ii* Bom. עֲלַם. *kk* Bom. וְאַפֵּישׁ. *ll* Bom. וְאַסְגֵי. *mm* B's reading תְּרֵין appears preferable when compared with the Hebrew שְׁנֵים. *nn* Bom. וְאֶתְּנִנֵיהּ.

(21) יָת קׇרְבְּנֵי אַקְרֵיב עִם יִצְחָק דְּתַלְיָ֯א לָךְ טוּרָא דְתַלְיָ֯א לָךְ טוּרָא דִּסְמֹאלָא
הֲדֵין בְּסֵא אַחֲלוֹחָא

(22) וְשַׁוְשֵׁי מֶטֶלְלָא עֲמֵיהּ וְאַשְׁלֵם קְצָרָא דְּרָ֯א מְעַלְוֹחֵי
דְאַבְרָהָם

(23) וּדְבַר אַבְרָהָם יָת יִשְׁמָעֵאל בְּרֵיהּ יָת כָּל יְלִידֵי בֵּיתֵיהּ
וְיָת כָּל זְבִינֵי כַּסְפֵּיהּ כָּל דְּכוּרָ֯א בֵּית אַבְרָהָם וּגְזַר יָת
בִּסְרָא דְעׇרְלָתְהוֹן בְּכֵן יוֹמָא הָדֵין כְּמָא דְמַלֵּיל עֲמֵיהּ יְיָ

(24) וְאַבְרָהָם בַּר תִּשְׁעִין וּתְשַׁע שְׁנִין כַּד גְּזַר בִּסְרָא
דְעׇרְלָתֵיהּ

(25) וְיִשְׁמָעֵאל בְּרֵיהּ בַּר תְּלַת עֲסַר שְׁנִין כַּד גְּזַר יָת בִּסְרָא
דְעׇרְלָתֵיהּ

(26) בְּכֵן יוֹמָא הָדֵין אִתְגְּזַר אַבְרָהָם וְיִשְׁמָעֵאל בְּרֵיהּ

(27) וְכָל אֱנָשֵׁי בֵּיתֵיהּ יְלִידֵי בֵּיתָא וּזְבִינֵי כַּסְפָּא מִן בַּר
עַמְמַיָּא אִתְגְּזַרוּ עֲמֵיהּ

CHAPTER XXVI.

(1) וַהֲוָה כַּפְנָא בְּאַרְעָא וַאֲזַל בְּמִצְרַיִם בַּר מִכַּפְנָא קַדְמָאָה דַּהֲוָה בְּיוֹמֵי
אַבְרָהָם וַאֲזַל יִצְחָק לְוָת אֲבִימֶלֶךְ מַלְכָּא דִפְלִשְׁתָּאֵי לִגְרָר

(2) וְאִתְגְּלִי לֵיהּ יְיָ וַאֲמַר לָא תֵיחוֹת לְמִצְרַיִם שְׁרֵי
בְּאַרְעָא דְאֵימַר לָךְ

a B, C אֲבָא, A אֲבֵי. The best form would be אֲבָא.
b Bom. דִּי תְלִי. *c* Bom. חֲדָא, B חֲדָא. *d* Bom. אַתְרַיָּא, A
אַתְרָא, B אַתְרָא, C אַתְרַיָּא. *e* Bom. שַׁוֵּי. *f* B מְטַלְלָא,
Ber. כַּלְדָּא. *g* Bom. מְעַלֵּי. *h* Bom. בְּאָתַר, A בְּאָתַר.
i A יְלִידֵיהּ, Bom. יְלִידֵיהּ. *k* Bom. כָּל דְּ רָ. *l* Bom.
עֲשַׁר. *m* דְעׇרְלָתֵיהּ. *n* קְדָם (B. on the other hand has בַּר
and also גְּבַר for אֲנָשֵׁי in verse 27). *o* Bom. אִתַּר. *p* Bom.
אִתְרַע. *q* בֵּ would be a better punctuation. *r* Bom.
קַדְמָא. *s* Bom. זְנֵי. *t* Bom. דַאֲבֵי. *u* B בְּמִצְרַיִם. *x* Bom.
שְׁרֵי. *y* A דְאֵימָר(!)

(3) דּוֹר בְּאַרְעָא הֲדָא וִיהֵי מֵימְרִי בְּסַעֲדָךְ וְאַבְרְגֵךְ אֲרֵי
לָךְ וְלִבְנָךְ אֶתֵּין יָת כָּל אַרְעָתָא הָאִלֵּין וַאֲקִים יָת קְיָמָא
דְּקַיֵּימִית לְאַבְרָהָם אֲבוּךְ
(4) וְאַסְגֵּי יָת בְּנָךְ כְּכוֹכְבֵי שְׁמַיָּא וְאֶתֵּין לִבְנָךְ יָת כָּל
אַרְעָתָא הָאִלֵּין וְיִתְבָּרְכוּן בְּדִיל בְּנָךְ כֹּל עַמְמֵי אַרְעָא
(5) חֲלָף דְּקַבִּיל אַבְרָהָם בְּמֵימְרִי וּנְטַר מַטְּרַת מֵימְרִי
פִּקּוּדַי קְיָמַי וְאוֹרָיָתָי
(6) וִיתֵיב יִצְחָק בִּגְרָר
(7) וּשְׁאִילוּ אֱנָשֵׁי אַתְרָא עַל עִסַּק אִתְּתֵיהּ וַאֲמַר אֲחָת
הִיא אֲרֵי דְחִיל לְמֵימַר אִתְּתִי דִּלְמָא יִקְטְלוּנַנִי אֱנָשֵׁי אַתְרָא
עַל רִבְקָה אֲרֵי שַׁפִּירַת חֵיזוּ הִיא
(8) וַהֲוָה כַּד סְגִיאוּ לֵיהּ תַּמָּן יוֹמַיָּא וְאִסְתְּכֵי אֲבִימֶלֶךְ
מַלְכָּא דִפְלִשְׁתָּאֵי מִן חֲרַכָּא וַחֲזָא וְהָא יִצְחָק מְחָיֵךְ עִם
רִבְקָה אִתְּתֵיהּ
(9) וּקְרָא אֲבִימֶלֶךְ לְיִצְחָק וַאֲמַר בְּרַם הָא אִתְּתָךְ הִיא
וְאֵיכְדֵין אֲמַרְתְּ אֲחָת הִיא וַאֲמַר לֵיהּ יִצְחָק אֲרֵי אֲמָרִית
דִּלְמָא אִתְקְטִיל עֲלַהּ
(10) וַאֲמַר אֲבִימֶלֶךְ מָא דָא עֲבַדְתְּ לָנָא כִּזְעֵיר פּוֹן
שָׁכֵיב דִּמְיַחַד בְּעַלְמָא יָת אִתְּתָךְ וְאַיְתִיתָא עֲלָנָא חוֹבָא

a Bom. יְהֵי. *b* Bom. בְּסַעֲדָּךְ. *c* Bom. וַאֲבָרְדִינָךְ. *d* Bom. אֲחֵן. *e* Bom. אַרְעָא. *f* Bom. וַאֲקַיֵּים (correctly). *g* C קָדְלָא. *h* Bom. בְּדָךְ. *i* Bom. וְאֶתֵּן. *k* Bom. לִבְדָךְ. *l* Bom. אַרְעָא. *m* Bom. עַמְמֵי. *n* Bom. קַבֵּיל. *o* Bom. מַטְרֵהּ. *p* Bom. פִּקּוֹדַי. *q* B קְיָמַי. *r* Bom. וְאוֹרָיְתֵי. *B* וְאוֹרָיְתָאֵי. *s* Bom. וְיָתֵיב. *t* Bom. אֲנָשֵׁי. *u* Bom. עִסְקָא. *x* Bom. אֲחָתִי. *y* Bom. דָּחֵיל. *z* Bom. אֲנָשֵׁי. *aa* Bom. רִבְקָה (and not רִבְקָא as B.). *bb* Bom. סְגִיאוּ. *cc* וְאִסְתְּכֵי would be a better reading. *dd* Bom. מְחָיֵךְ, C חָאֵךְ. *ee* Bom. עִם (B. has עֵם). *ff* Bom. וַאֲמַר. *gg* Bom. אֲחָת, *h* אֲמָרֵית. *hh* Bom. אֲמַרִית. *ii* Bom. אֲמָרִית. *kk* Bom. אִתְקְטֵיל correctly; also C אִתְקְטִיל. *ll* Bom. בַּהּ דָּא. *mm* Bom. עֲבַדְתְּ. *nn* Bom. לָנָא, C לָנָה. *oo* Cf. LXX which has ἐκ τοῦ γένους μου. *pp* Bom. יָת. *qq* Bom. אַיְתִיתָא. The best reading would be וְאַיְתִיתָא.

(11) יַעֲקֹד אֲבִישְׁלָךְ יָת שְׁמָא דְּמָרֵי עָלְמָא בְּמֵימְרֵהּ דְּחִזְדָּק[a] אֶתְקְטִיל[c] לְנִגְבָּא[b]
הָדֵין לְוַלְגֵרָיָהּ[d] אֶתְקְטִיל הַקְטֵיל[d]

(12) יְדַע יִצְחָק בְּאַרְעָא הַהִיא וְאַשְׁכַּח בְּשַׁתָּא הַהִיא עַל חַד
מְאָה בְּהִסְתַּרְוָתִי[e] וּבְרָכַהּ יְיָ

(13) וּרְבָא גַּבְרָא וְאָזֵיל[g] אָזֵיל וְרָבֵי[h] עַד דַּרְבָא[k] לַחֲדָא

(14) וַהֲוִי[l] לֵיהּ גֵּיתֵי[m] עָנָא גֵּיתֵי תוֹרֵי וּפָלְחָנָא[o] סַגִי
וְקַנִּיאוּ בֵּיהּ פְּלִשְׁתָּאֵי[p]

(15) וְכָל בֵּירֵי[q] דַּחֲפָרוּ[d] עַבְדֵי אֲבוּהִי[r] בְּיוֹמֵי אַבְרָהָם אֲבוּהִי
טְמוֹנִינוּן[t] פְּלִשְׁתָּאֵי וּמְלוֹנִינוּן[u] עַפְרָא

(16) אֲמַר[x] אֲבִימֶלֶךְ לְיִצְחָק אִיזֵיל[y] מִלְּוָתָנָא[z] אֲרֵי תְּקֵיפַת[a]
מִלָּנָא לַחֲדָא[aa]

(17) וְאָזֵל מִתַּמָּן[bb] יִצְחָק וּשְׁרָא בְּחִלָּא דִגְרָר וְיָתֵיב[cc] תַּמָּן

(18) וְתָב יִצְחָק וְחַפַּר יָת בֵּירֵי[dd] דְּמַיָא[ee] דַּחֲפָרוּ[ee] בְּיוֹמֵי
אַבְרָהָם אֲבוּהִי וּטְמוֹנִינוּן[ff] פְּלִשְׁתָּאֵי[gg] בָּתַר דְּמִית אַבְרָהָם וּקְרָא
לְהֵן[hh] שְׁמָהָן כִּשְׁמָהָן[ii] דַּהֲוָה[jj] קְרֵי לְהֵן[kk] אֲבוּהִי[ll]

(19) וַחֲפָרוּ עַבְדֵי יִצְחָק בְּחִלָּא וְאַשְׁכָּחוּ[mm] תַּמָּן בֵּיר[nn]
דְּמַיִין[oo] נָבְעִין[pp]

---

a Bom. דְּחִזְדָּק. *b* Bom. לְגַבָּא. *c* Bom. הִתְקְטֵל.
d C לְוַלְגֵרָיָהּ. *e* Bom. דְּחִי. *f* Bom. בִּשְׁבָלִין. *g* Bom. אָזַל.
h B has this word added on the margin. B. omits it.
i Bom. רָבָא. *k* Bom. דִּרְבָא. *l* Bom. וַהֲוָה C הֲוָה. *m* Bom.
גֵיתֵי. *n* Bom. תוֹרֵי. *o* Bom. וּפוּלְחָנָא. *A* has this word
erased in the text but added on the margin; whilst *B* has
it in the text and עַבְדִּין on the margin. *p* B וְקַנִּיאוּ.
q Bom. בֵּירִין, B בֵּירָא. *r* Bom. דַּחֲפַר לֵהּ. *s* Bom. אֲבוּהִי.
t Bom. טְמוֹנוּן and Raši quotes the word thus. *u* Bom. וּמְלוֹנוּן.
x Bom. וַאֲמַר. *y* Bom. אֱזֵיל. *z* Bom. מִלְּוָתָנָא, C דִּילָנָא.
aa Bom. תְּקֵפַת. *bb* Bom. תַּמָּן. *cc* Bom. וִיתֵב. *dd* Bom. בֵּירָא.
B בֵּירָא. *ee* Bom. דְּמַיָא. *ff* Bom. אֲבוּהִי. *gg* Bom. וּטְמוֹנוּן.
The best reading would be וּטְמוֹנוּן. *hh* Bom. לְהוֹן (B. לְהֵין.
ii Bom. כִּשְׁמָהָן. *kk* C has קְרָא instead of קְרֵי הֲוָה. *ll* Bom.
אֲבוּהִי. *mm* C וְאַשְׁכַּח, A וְאַשְׁכָּחוּ. *nn* Bom. בֵּירָא. *oo* Bom.
דְּמַיִין. *pp* Bom. נָבְעִין.

(20) וּנְצִי רֹעוֹתָאa דִּגְרַר עִם רֹעוֹתָא דְיִצְחָק בְּמֵימַר דִּילֵהּb
אֲלָא וּקְרָא שְׁמֵהּc דְּבֵירָא עֵסֶק אֲרֵי אִתְעַסְּקוּd עִמֵּהּ
(21) וַחֲפַרוּ בֵירa אָחֳרִיf וּנְצוֹ אַף עֲלַהּ וּקְרָא שְׁמַהּ שִׂטְנָה
(22) וְאִסְתַּלַּק מִתַּמָּן וְחָפַר בֵּירg אָחֳרִיh וְלָא נְצוֹ עֲלַהּ וּקְרָא
שְׁמַהּ רְחוֹבוֹתi וַאֲמַרk אֲרֵי כְּעַן אַפְתִּי יְיָ לָנָא וְנֵיפּוֹשׁl בְּאַרְעָא
(23) וְאִסְתַּלַּקm מִתַּמָּן לִבְאֵר שָׁבַע
(24) וְאִתְגְּלִיn לֵיהּ יְיָ בְּלֵילְיָא הַהוּא וַאֲמַר אֲנָא אֱלָהֵהּo
דְּאַבְרָהָם אֲבוּךְp לָא תִדְחַל אֲרֵי בְסַעְדָּךְq מֵימְרִיr וְאַבְרְכִנָּךְs וְאַסְגֵי
יָת בְּנָךְ בְּדִיל אַבְרָהָם עַבְדִּי
(25) וּבְנָא תַמָּן מַדְבְּחָאs וְצַלִּי בִּשְׁמָא דַיְיָ וּפְרָסֵיהּ תַּמָּן
לְמַשְׁכְּנֵיהּt וַחֲפַרוּ תַמָּן עַבְדֵי יִצְחָק בֵּירָא
(26) וַאֲבִימֶלֶךְ אֲתָאu לְוָתֵיהּ מִגְּרָר וְסִיעַתx רָחֲמוֹהִיy
וּפִיכֹל רַב חֵילֵיהּ
(27) וַאֲמַרz לְהוֹן יִצְחָק מָדֵין אֲתֵיתוֹןbb לְוָתִי וְאַתּוּן
סְנֵיתוּן יָתִי וְשַׁלַּחְתּוּנִי מִלְּוָתְכוֹןcc
(28) וַאֲמַרוּdd מֶחֱזָאee חֲזֵינָא אֲרֵי הֲוָהff מֵימְרָא דַיְיָ
בְּסַעְדָּךְgg וַאֲמַרְנָא תִתְקַיֵּםhh כְּעַן מוֹמָתָא דַּהֲוַת בֵּין אֲבָהָתָנָאii
בֵינָנָא וּבֵינָךְ וְנִגְזַר קְיָם עִמָּךְ

---

a Bom. רַעְיָתָא. *b* Bom. דִּילָהּ. *c* Bom. שְׁמָא. *d* Bom. אִתְעַסְּקוּ. *e* Bom. בֵירָא. *f* A, B, C אוֹחֳרִי, Bom. אוֹחֳרֵי. The Šewa compositum given by D is irregular in the Spl. vocalization; אָחֳרִי would be the best reading. *g* Bom. בֵּירָא. *h* A, B, C אוֹחֳרִי, Bom. אוֹחֳרֵי. *i* C רְחוֹבֹת. *k* Bom. וַאֲמַר. *l* A, B (more correctly) וְנִיפּוּשׁ and וְנִיפֵּישׁ. *m* Bom. וְסָלִיק. B, C (more correctly) סְלֵיק. *n* B וְאִיתְגְּלִי. *o* Bom. אֱלָהָא. *p* Bom. אֲבוּךָ. *q* Bom. בְּסַעְדָּךְ. *r* Bom. וַאֲבָרְכִינָךְ. *s* Bom. מַדְבְּחָא. *t* Bom. מַשְׁכְּנֵיהּ. *u* Bom. אֲזַל, A אֲתֵי. *x* A רְחִישָׁא. *y* Bom. רָחֲמוֹהִי, A, B רַחֲמֵיהּ, and the word is thus quoted in Gen. Rabb. c. 64 § 9 (in Wilna Edition). *z* Bom. וַאֲמַר. *aa* Bom. מָה דֵּין. *bb* Bom. אֲתֵיתוּן. *cc* Bom. מִלְּוָתְכוֹן. *dd* Bom. וַאֲמַר. *ee* Bom. מֶחֱזָא. *ff* Bom. הֲוָה. *gg* Bom. בְּסַעְדָּךְ. *hh* Bom. תִּתְקַיֵּם. *ii* Bom. אֲבָהָתָנָא.

(29) אִם תַּעֲבֵיד[a] עִמָּא דִּלָא בְּמָא בְּרִישָׁא אַנְוִיקוּנָךְ[b] וּכְמָא דְעָבַדְנָא[c] עִמָךְ דְּחוּד טָב דְּשַׁלַחְתּוּן בִּשְׁלָם אַף כֵּן בְּעָן בְּרִיכָא דְּיִי
(30) וּכְבַד[d] כְּהוּן מַשְׁחָא[e] וַאֲכַלוּ[f] וְיִשְׂרָאֵל[g]
(31) וְאַקְדִימוּ בְּצַפְרָא וְקַיִימוּ לַאֲחוּהִי[h] בַּר לַאֲחוּהִי וְשַׁלְּחִינוּן[i] יִצְחָק וְאָזַלוּ[k] מִלְוָתֵיהּ בִּשְׁלָם
(32) וַהֲוָה בְּיוֹמָא הַהוּא וְאָתוֹ[l] עַבְדֵי יִצְחָק וְחַוִּיאוּ לֵיהּ עַל עֵיסַק[m] בֵּירָא דְחַפָרוּ[n] וַאֲמָרוּ[o] לֵיהּ אַשְׁכַּחְנָא מַיָּא
(33) וְקָרָא יָתַהּ שִׁבְעָה[p] עַל כֵּן שְׁמָהּ[q] דְּקַרְתָּא בְּאֵר שֶׁבַע עַד יוֹמָא הָדֵין
(34) וַהֲוָה עֵשָׂו בַּר אַרְבְּעִין שְׁנִין וּנְסִיב אִתְּתָא יָת יְהוּדִית בַּת בְּאֵרִי חִתָּאָה וְיָת בָּסְמַת בַּת אֵילוֹן חִתָּאָה
(35) וַהֲוָאָה מַסְרְבָן וּמַרְגְּזָן[s] עַל מֵימַר יִצְחָק וְרִבְקָה

CHAPTER XXXI.

(1) וּשְׁמַע יָת פִּתְגָּמֵי בְנֵי לָבָן דְּאָמְרִין[t] נְסִיב[u] יַעֲקֹב יָת כָּל דִּלְאַבוּנָא[x] וּמִדִּלְאַבוּנָא[y] קְנָא יָת כָּל יְקָרָא הָדֵין
(2) וַחֲזָא יַעֲקֹב יָת סְבַר אַפֵּי לָבָן וְהָא לֵיתֵינוּן[z] עִמֵּיהּ בְּמָאתְמָלֵי[aa] וּמִקַּדְמוֹהִי

a Bom. תַּעֲבֵיד. *b* Bom. אַנְוִיקוּנָךְ. *c* Bom. דִּי־עֲבַדְנָא, B אִבדנא. *d* Bom. וְכַד. *e* Bom. מַשְׁיָא, C בְּשִׁתְלָא. *f* Bom. וְאָכַל. *g* C וְיִשְׂרָאֵל. *h* B בֵּיהּ instead of בַּר לַאֲחוּהִי. Bom. אַחְתֵּיהּ. *i* Bom. וְשַׁלְּחִינוּן, B שַׁלַחְתִּנוּן. *k* Bom. וְאָזַל. *l* Bom. וָאֲתָא. *m* Bom. עֵסַק. *n* Bom. דִּי־חֲפָרוּ. *o* Bom. וָאֲמָרוּ. *p* Bom. שִׁבְעָה (and not as B. שַׁבְעָה). This is likewise the Bib. Aram. form. Cf. Daniel 4, 13. *q* Bom. שְׁבָא. *r* Bom. יְדַעְנָא. *s* Bom. וְרִבְקָה (and not as B. וְרִבְקָה). *t* A Bom. דְּאָמְרִין. So also B לִמֵימַר (which is better than D). *u* Bom. נְסַב. *x* Bom. דִּי־לְאָבוּנָא. *y* Bom. וּמֵדְבַר לְאָבִינוּ. *z* Bom. בְּיִצְחָק, C (text) לַבָּן. On the margin לְוָתֵיהּ. *aa* Bom. בְּמֶאתְמָלֵי, C כְּבֵאתְמָלֵי (which is better than D).

(3) וַאֲמַר֫ יְיָ לְיַעֲקֹב תּוּב לְאַרְעָ֫א אֲבָהָתָ֫ךְ֫ וְלִילְדוּתָ֫ךְ֫
וִיהֵ֫י מֵימְרִי בְּסַעְדָּ֫ךְ

(4) וּשְׁלַח יַעֲקֹב וּקְרָ֫א לְרָחֵל וְלֵלֵאָ֫ה לְחַקְלָ֫א לְוָת עָנֵיהּ

(5) וַאֲמַר֫ לְהֹון֫ חָזֵ֫י אֲנָ֫א יָת סְבַר אַפֵּי אֲבוּכֵן֫ אֲרֵי
לֵיתִיהוֹן֫ עִמִּי כְּמֵאֶתְמָלִי, וּמִקַּדְמוֹהִי וֶאֱלָהֵיהּ דְּאַבָּא הֲוָה
בְּסַעְדִּי

(6) וְאַתֵּין֫ וְלֵעְתִּין֫ אֲרֵי בְּכֹל חֵילִי פְּלֵחִית֫ יָת אֲבוּכֵן֫

(7) וַאֲבוּכוֹן֫ שַׁקַּר֫ בִּי וְאַשְׁנִי יָת אַגְרִי עֲשַׂר זִמְנִין וְלָא
שַׁבְקֵיהּ יְיָ לְאַבְאָשָׁא עִמִּי

(8) אִם כְּדֵין הֲוָה אָמַר֫ נְמוֹרִין יְהֵי אַגְרָךְ וִילִידָן כָּל
עָנָא נְמוֹרִין וְאִם כְּדֵין הֲוָה אָמַר רְגוֹלִין יְהֵי אַגְרָךְ וִילִידָן כָּל
עָנָא רְגוֹלִין

(9) וְאַפְרֵישׁ יְיָ מִן בְּעִירָא דַּאֲבוּכוֹן וִיהַב לִי

(10) וַהֲוָה בְּעִדָּן דְּאִתְיַחֲמָא עָנָא וּזְקָפִית עֵינַי וַחֲזִית
בְּחֶלְמָא וְהָא תֵּישַׁיָּא דְּסָלְקִין עַל עָנָא רְגוֹלִין נְמוֹרִין
וּפְצִיחִין

(11) וַאֲמַר לִי מַלְאֲכָא דַּייָ בְּחֶלְמָא יַעֲקֹב וַאֲמָר הָאֲנָא

(12) וַאֲמַר זְקוֹף כְּעַן עֵינָךְ וַחֲזִי כָּל תֵּישַׁיָּא דְּסָלְקִין

---

a Bom. יָאֲמַר. *b* Bom. לְאַרְעָא. *c* Bom. אֲבָהָתָךְ. *d* Bom. וְלִילְדוּתָךְ. *e* Bom. יְהֵי. *f* Bom. חַקְלָא. *g* Bom. עָנֵהּ. *h* Bom. לְהֵין (B. לְהֵין). *i* Bom. חָזִי. *k* Bom. אֲבוּכֵן, C אֲבוּכֵן. *l* B הָא. *m* Bom. לְיָתְהוֹן, which is the best reading. *n* Bom. יָאתוּן. *o* Bom. יְדַעְתָּן. *p* Bom. פְּלֵחִית. *q* Bom. אֲבוּכֵן (B. אֲבוּכֵן). *r* Bom. יָאשְׁנֵי (B. יָאֲבוּכוֹן). *s* Bom. שַׁקַר. *t* Bom. יָאשְׁנֵי. *u* B עֲשַׂר. *v* Bom. אֲגַר. *y* Bom. וִילִידָן (the best reading would be יְלִידָן). *z* Bom. יָאֲפֵי. *aa* Instead of בְּעִירָא דְ, Bom. reads עָנָא. *bb* Bom. דַּאֲבוּכֵן. *cc* B. דְּאִתְיָחֲדָא. *dd* Bom. יַחֲזִית. *ee* Bom. בְּחֶלְמָא. *ff* Bom. תֵּישָׁיָא. *gg* A דְּסָלְקִין, B הָסָלְקִין. *hh* Bom. וּפְצִיחִין. *ii* Bom. יָאֲמָר. *kk* Bom. בְּחֶלְמָא. *ll* Bom. יָאֲמַר. *mm* A, C עֵינַי and עֵינָךְ. *nn* Bom. וַחֲזִי. *oo* Bom. תֵּישָׁיָא.

עַל פָּמָא דְגִלְיוֹן בְמוֹדִין לְפָּטִיחִין^a אֲרֵי גַלֵי קָדָמַי יָת כָּל דְעָבַד^b
לָבָן.

(13) אֲנָא אֱלָהָא^c דְאִתְגְלֵיתִי^d עֲלָךְ בְּבֵית^e אֵל דְמַשְחַתָא^f
תַמָן קָמָא דְקַיְמְתָא^h קָדָמַי תַמָן קַיָם בְסַן פּוּק^i מִן אַרְעָא
הָדָא^k וְתִיב לְאַרַע יַלָדוּתָךְ.^{l}

(14) וַאֲתִיבַת^m רָחֵל וְלֵאָה וְאָמְרַן^n לֵיהּ הַעַד^o כְעַן לָנָא
חוּלָק וְאַחֲסָנָא^p בְבֵית אַבוּנָא.^{q}

(15) הֲלָא נוּכְרָאָן^r אִתְחַשַבְנָא^s לֵיהּ אֲרֵי זַבְנָנָא וַאֲכַל אַף
מֵיכַל יָת כַסְפָנָא.

(16) אֲרֵי כָל עוּתְרָא^u דְאַפְרֵישׁ^{x} יְיָ מִן אֲבוּנָא^y דִילָנָא^z
הוּא וְדִבְנָנָא^{aa} וּכְעַן כָל דַאֲמַר^{bb} יְיָ לָךְ עֲבֵיד.

(17) קָם יַעֲקֹב וּנְטַל יָת בְנוֹהִי וְיָת נְשׁוֹהִי עַל גַמְלַיָא.

(18) וּדְבַר יָת כָל גֵיתוֹהִי^{cc} וְיָת כָל קִנְיָנֵיהּ דְקָנָא גֵיתוּהִי
וּקְנַיָנֵיהּ דִקְנָא בְפַדַן אֲרָם^{dd} לְמֵיתֵי לְוָת יִצְחָק אֲבוּהִי לְאַרְעָא
דִכְנָעַן.

(19) וְלָבָן אֲזַל לְמֵיגַז^{ee} יָת עָנֵיהּ וּנְסֵיבַת^{gg} רָחֵל יָת
צַלְמַנָיָא דְלַאֲבוּהָא.^{hh}

(20) וְכַסִי^{ii} יַעֲקֹב מִן לָבָן אֲרַמָאָה עַל דְלָא חַוִי^{kk} לֵיהּ אֲרֵי
אָזִיל הוּא.

---

a Bom. וּפְגִיעִין. *b* Bom. דְעָ-. *c* Bom. אֱלָהָא. *d* Bom. דְאִ-לֵי-תִי. *e* C בֵ-. *f* Bom. מְשַחְ-תָ. *g* B inserts דְבֵית before אֵל. *h* Bom. קַיָמְ-תָּ. *i* Bom. פּוּק. *k* C reads הָדָה אַרְעָא instead of הָדָא אַרְעָא. *l* Bom. יַלְדוּ-תָ. *m* Bom. יַעֲנַת. The correct form is אֲתִיבַת. *n* Bom. וַאֲמַרָן, A וַאֲמַרָן. *o* Bom. הַעוֹד. *p* Bom. וַאֲחַסָ-נָא. *q* Bom. אַבָּא. *r* Bom. נוּכְרָאָן, B לָאָ-לָ-. *s* Bom. אַחְשַבְנָא. *t* Bom. זַבְנַנְ. *u* Bom. עוּתְרָ. *x* B אתרא which is preferable. *y* B אַבוּנָא. *z* Bom. דִילַן. *aa* Bom. וְדִבְנָ-נָא. *bb* Bom. דַ אֲמַר. *cc* Bom. גֵיתוֹ-הִי. *dd* Bom. אֲרָם. *ee* Bom. מֵיגַז. *ff* Bom. עֲנֵ-הּ. *gg* Bom. וְנָסֵ-בַת. *hh* Bom. אֲבוּהָ -ד. *ii* Bom. וְכַסִי. *kk* Bom. חַוִי.

(21) וַאֲזַל֩ הוּא וְכָל דְּלֵיהּ וְקָם דְּעֲבַר יָת פְּרָת וְשַׁוִּי
יָת אַפּוֹהִי לְטוּרָא דְגִלְעָד

(22) וְאִתַּחֲוָא לְלָבָן בְּיוֹמָא תְלִיתָאָה אֲרֵי אֲזַל יַעֲקֹב

(23) וּדְבַר יָת אֲחוֹהִי עִמֵּיהּ וּרְדַף בַּתְרוֹהִי מַהֲלַךְ שִׁבְעָא
יוֹמִין וְאַדְבִּיק יָתֵיהּ בְּטוּרָא דְגִלְעָד

(24) וַאֲתָא מֵימַר מִן קֳ(דָם) יְיָ לְוָת לָבָן אֲרַמָּאָה בְּחֶלְמָא
דְלֵילְיָא וַאֲמַר לֵיהּ אִסְתַּמַּר לָךְ דִּלְמָא תְמַלֵּיל עִם יַעֲקֹב מִטָּב
עַד בִּישׁ

(25) וְאַדְבִּיק לָבָן יָת יַעֲקֹב וְיַעֲקֹב פְּרַס יָת מַשְׁכְּנֵיהּ
בְּטוּרָא וְלָבָן אַשְׁרִי יָת אֲחוֹהִי בְּטוּרָא דְגִלְעָד

(26) וַאֲמַר לָבָן לְיַעֲקֹב מָא עֲבַדְתָּא וְכַסִּיתָא מִנִּי
וּדְבַרְתָּ יָת בְּנָתַי כִּשְׁבַיַת חַרְבָּא

(27) לְמָא טְמַרְתָּא לְמֵיזַל וְכַסִּיתָא מִנִּי דְלָא חַוִּית לִי
וְשַׁלַּחְתָּךְ אִין בְּחֶדְוָא וּבְתֻשְׁבְּחָן בְּתוּפִין וּבְכִנָּרִין

(28) וְלָא שַׁבַקְתַּנִי לְנַשָּׁקָא לִבְנַי וְלִבְנָתַי כְּעַן אַסְכֵּלְתָּא לְמֶעְבַּד

(29) אִית חֵילָא בִּידִי לְמֶעְבַּד עִמְּכוֹן בִּישָׁא וֵאלָהָא

a Bom. וַאֲזַל. *b* Bom. דִּי לֵיהּ. *c* Bom. וַעֲבַר. *d* B דִּנְהַר
פְּרָת which is better. *e* Bom. בְּמֵישְׁרָא, C בְּשָׁלָא. *f* אַחְוִי
would be a better reading. *g* B שַׁבְעָא. *h* Bom. וְאַדְבִּיק.
i Bom. בְּחֵילְקָא. *k* The correct text should be אִסְתְּמַר. *l* Bom.
אֲמַר. *m* Bom. אֲחוֹהִי. *n* Bom. וַאֲמַר. *o* Bom. מָה. *p* Bom.
עֲבַדְתְּ. *q* Bom. וְכַסִּיתָא. *r* Bom. וּדְבַרְתָּא, A וּדְבַרְתְּ, B דַּהֲוָה.
s Bom. בְּנָי (B. בְּנָתַי), B בְּנַי. *t* Bom. בְּשִׁבְיָא, A בְּשִׁבְיָא.
The best reading would be שְׁבַבְלָא. *u* Bom. חַרְבָּא. *x* Bom.
אִטְמַרְתָּא, A אִטְמַרְתָּא. *y* Bom. וְכַסִּיתָא. *z* A, B הֲוִית. The best reading would perhaps be חַוֵּית. *aa* Bom. וְשַׁלַּחְתָּךְ, A, B וְאַשְׁלַחְתָּךְ.
bb Bom. adds זִמְן before בְּחֶדְוָא. *C* has the same word here
whilst *B* and *D* insert it on the margin. Vide Barth in
ZDMG. XXX, p. 190. *cc* Bom. בְּחֶדְוָא. *dd* Bom. יִבְתֻשְׁבְּחָן.
ee Bom. וּבְכִנָּרִין, A וּבְכִנָּרִין. *ff* שַׁבַּקְתַּנִי. *gg* Bom. אַסְכֵּלְתָּא.
hh Bom. לְמֶעְבַּד. *ii* Bom. לְמֶעְבַּד. *kk* Bom. בִּישׁ. *ll* Bom.
וֵאלָהָא (B. וֵאלָהָא), A, B וֵאלָהָא.

— 89 —

דְאָבִילְןָ בְחֶמְשָׁא אָמַר לֵיהª לִשִׁימֵר אֶסְחְמַר לָךְ מִלְמַלָלָאᵇ עִם
יַעֲקֹב מִטָב עַד בִּישׁ

(30) וּכְעַן מֵיזַל אָזַלְחָאᶜ אֲרֵי חֶמְדָא חֲמֵידְחָאᵈ לְבֵית אֲבוּךְ
לָמָא נְסֵיבְחָא יָת דַּחֲלָחֵיᵉ

(31) וְאֲתִיבᶠ יַעֲקֹב וְאָמַרᵍ לְלָבָן אֲרֵי דְחִילִיחʰ אֲרֵי אֲמָרִיתⁱ
דִילְמָא תִּנְסֵיסᵏ יָת בְּנָחָךְ מִנִּי

(32) עִם דִּיׁחַשְׁכַּחִ׳ יָת דַחֲלָחָךְᵐ לָא יִחְקַיֵּםⁿ קֳדָם אַחֲנָא
אִשְׁחְמוֹדַע לָךְ מָאᵒ דְּעִמִּי סַב לָךְ וְלָא יְדַעᵖ יַעֲקֹב אֲרֵי רָחֵל
נְסֵיבַחְחוּןᑫ

(33) וְעַל לָבָן בְּמַשְׁכְּנָא דְיַעֲקֹב וּבְמַשְׁכְּנָא דְלֵאָה וּבְמַשְׁכְּנָא
דְתַרְחֵין לְחִינָחָא וְלָא אַשְׁכַּח וּנְפַק מִמַּשְׁכְּנָא דְלֵאָה וְעַל בְמַשְׁכְּנָא
דְרָחֵל

(34) וְרָחֵל נְסֵיבַת יָת צַלְמָנַיָא וְשַׁוִּיאָחְנוּןˢ בְּעָבִיטָא דְגַמְלָא
וִיתֵיבַת עֲלֵיהוֹן וּמַשֵּׁישᵘ לָבָן יָת כָּל מַשְׁכְּנָא וְלָא אַשְׁכַּח

(35) וְאַמְרַתˣ לְאַבוּחָאʸ לָא יִחְקַףᶻ בְּעֵינֵי רִבּוֹנִי אֲרֵי לָא
אִיכוּלᵃᵃ לִמְקָםᵇᵇ מִן קֳדָמָךְ אֲרֵי אוֹרַח נְשִׁין לִי וּבְלַשׁ וְלָא
אַשְׁכַּח יָת צַלְמָנַיָּא

(36) וּחְקִיףᶜᶜ לְיַעֲקֹב וּנְצָא עִם לָבָן וְאָתִיבᵈᵈ יַעֲקֹב וְאָמַרᵉᵉ
לְלָבָן מָאᶠᶠ חוֹבִי מָא סוּרְחָנִיᵍᵍ אֲרֵי רְדַפְחָא בַּחְרָיʰʰ

a B has אֲמַר לֵ׳ בְ׳ in the text, but margin as above.
b C Text לְמַלָלָא אִלָּא. Margin as above. *c* Bom. אֲזַלְחְּ.
d Bom. חַמְדְּחָא. *e* Bom. דַּחֲלְחֵי. *f* Bom. וַאֲחֵיב. *g* Bom. אֲמַר.
h Bom. דְחִלְיַח. *i* Bom. אֲמַרִיח. *k* Bom. חֵיסַב. *l* Bom. דְּ
חֵשְׁכַּח. *m* Bom. דַחֲלְחָךְ. *n* Bom. יִחְקַיֵים. *o* Bom. מַה.
p Bom. יְדַע (B. יְדַע). *q* Bom. נְסֵיבַחְהִינוּן. *r* Bom. נְסֵיבַח.
s Bom. וְשַׁוִּיחְנוּן, B לְשַׁוִּיתְנוּן. *t* Bom. וִיחֵיבַח. *u* B וּמַשֵּׁישׁ.
v Bom. וַאֲמֶרַח. *y* Bom. לְאַבִיחָא. *z* Bom. יִחְקַף. *aa* Bom.
אֵיכוּל, B אִיכֻל. *bb* Bom. לְמֶיקָם. *cc* Bom. adds רוּגְזָא after
וּחְקֵיף. *dd* Bom. וְאַחֵיב. *ee* Bom. אֲמַר. *ff* Bom. מַה.
gg Bom. סוּרְחָנוּ (B. סוּרְחָנִי). *hh* C בַּחְרַי.

(37) אֲרֵי מְשִׁישָׁא[a] יָת כָּל[b] מְנֵי מַא[c] אַשְׁכַּחְתָּא מִכָּל מָנֵי
בֵּיתָךְ שַׁו[d] הָכָא[e] קָ(דָם)[f] אֲחַי וְאַחָךְ וְיוֹכְחוּן בֵּין תַּרְוַלָא
(38) דְּנָן עֶסְרִין שְׁנִין אֲנָא עִמָּךְ רְחֵלָךְ[g] וְעִזָּךְ לָא אֲתַכִּלוּ[h]
וְדֶכְרֵי עָנָךְ לָא אֲכָלִית[h]
(39) דִּתְבִירָא[i] לָא אֵיתֵיתִי[k] לָךְ דְּחָת שַׁגְיָא[l] מִמִנְיָנָא[m] בְּעִי
אַתְּ בָעֵי לַהּ נְסְרִית[n] בִּימָמָא וּנְסְרִית בְּלֵילְיָא
(40) הֲוֵיתִי בִּימָמָא אֲכָלַנִי[o] שַׁרְבָּא[p] וְגִלִידָא נָחִית[q] עֲלַי[r]
בְּלֵילְיָא וּנְדָת[s] שִׁנְתִּי[t] מֵעֵינָי
(41) דְּנָן לִי עֶסְרִין[u] שְׁנִין בְּבֵיתָךְ פְּלַחְתָּךְ[x] אַרְבַּע עֶסְרֵי
שְׁנִין בְּתַרְתֵּין בְּנָתָךְ וְשִׁית[y] שְׁנִין בְּעָנָךְ וְאַשְׁנִיתָא[z] יָת אַגְרִי
עֲסַר זִמְנִין
(42) אִלוּלָא פוּן[aa] אֱלָהֵיהּ[bb] דְּאַבָּא אֱלָהֵיהּ דְּאַבְרָהָם
וּדְדָחִיל[cc] לֵיהּ יִצְחָק הֲוָה בְּסַעְדִי[dd] אֲרֵי כְּעַן רֵיקָם[ee] שַׁלַּחְתָּנִי[ff]
יָת עַמְלִי וְיָת לֵיאוּת[gg] יְדַי גְּלִי קָ(דָם) יְיָ אָזֵף בְּרַמְשָׁא
(43) וְאָתִיב[hh] לָבָן וַאֲמַר[ii] לְיַעֲקֹב בְּנָתָא בְּנָתִי[kk] וּבְנַיָּא בְּנַי[ll]

a Bom. מְשַׁשָׁא. *b* Bom. כָּל (B. כֹּל). *c* Bom. מָה. *d* Bom. שַׁוִּי which is preferable here. *e* B כָּה. *f* Bom. יָאָךְ. *g* Bom. רְחֵלָךְ. *h* Bom. אֲכָלִית. *i* Bom. תְּבִירָא, B דְּבִיר. *k* Bom. אֵיתִידַי. The best punctuation would be אֵיתִידַי. *l* The correct punctuation is שַׁגְיָא. *m* Bom. בְּמִנְיָנָא (B. בֵּן מִנְיָנָא), *A* בֵּן מִנְיָנָא, *B* מִן בֵּן. *n* Bom. נְסְרִיָּה. *o* Bom. אֲכָלַנִי. *p* Bom. שַׁרְבָא (but שַׁרְבָּא better). *q* Bom. נָחֵית (B. נָחִית). *A*, *B*, *C* נְחָת. *r* Bom. עֲלֵי. *s* Bom. וּנְדַת. *t* Bom. שַׁנְתִּי. *u* Bom. עֶסְרָיה (B. עֶסְרַיָּה). *x* Bom. פְּלַחְתָּךְ. *y* Bom. שִׁית. *z* Bom. וְאַשְׁנִיתָא. *aa* Bom. אִלְהוּלְפֵי. *bb* Bom. אֱלָהֵיהּ. *cc* Bom. שַׁלַּחְתָּנִי. *dd* Bom. בְּסַעְדִי. *ee* *A* רֵיקַן, *C* רֵיקָם. *ff* Bom. שַׁלַּחְתָּנִי, *C* שַׁלַּחְתֵּיהּ which is better. *gg* Bom. לֵיאָאת (B. לֵיאוּת). *hh* Bom. וַאֲתִיב but וְאָתִיב would be a better punctuation than that given by the Mss. *ii* Bom. וַאֲמַר. *kk* Bom. בְּנָתִי (B. בְּנָתַי). *ll* Bom. בְּנַי.

הָנָאᵃ בְּנֵיᵇ דְּבַל הָאֵת חֲזִיᶜ דִּילֵיᵈ הִיא דִּלְבְנָתֵיʳ מָאᶠ אִעֲבִיד
בָּאֲלֵין יוֹמָא דֵּין אִי לִבְנָתְהוֹןᵍ דִילְהוֹן

(44) וְכֵן אִיתָאʰ דַּאֲת יְאִיᵏ לְסָהִיד
בֵּינָא וּבֵינָךְ

(45) וּנְסֵיבᶫ יַעֲקֹב אַבְנָא וְזַקְפַּהᵐ קָמָא

(46) אָמַרⁿ יַעֲקֹב לְאַחְחוֹהִי לְקוּטוּ אַבְנִיןᵒ וּנְסִיבוּ אַבְנִין
וַעֲבַדᵖ דְּגוֹרָא⁹ וַאֲכַלוּ⁹ תַּמָּן עַל דְּגוֹרָא

(47) וּקְרָא לֵיהּ לָבָן יְגַר שַׂהֲדוּתָא וְיַעֲקֹב קְרָא לֵיהּ
גַּלְעֵד

(48) אָמַרˢ לָבָן דְּגוֹרָאᵗ הָדֵין סָהִיד בֵּינָאᵘ וּבֵינָךְ יוֹמָא
דֵין עַל כֵּן קְרָא שְׁמֵיהּ גַּלְעֵדˣ

(49) וְהַסְכוּתָאʸ דַּאֲמַרᶻ וְיֵסַךְ ᵃᵃ מֵימְרָא דַּיְיָ בֵּינָא וּבֵינָךְ אֲרֵי
נִתְכַּסֵּיᵇᵇ גְּבַר מֵחַבְרֵיהּ

(50) אִם תְּעַנֵּיᶜᶜ יָת בְּנָתִיᵈᵈ וְאִם תִּסַּב נְשִׁין עַל בְּנָתִי
לֵית אֱנָשᵉᵉ עִמָּנָא חֲזִי מֵימְרָא דַּיְיָ סָהִיד בֵּינָא וּבֵינָךְ

(51) אָמַרᶠ לָבָן לְיַעֲקֹב הָא דְגוֹרָא הָדֵין וְהָא קָמְתָאᶠᶠ
דַּאֲקֵימִיתᵍᵍ בֵּינָא וּבֵינָךְ

(52) סָהִיד דְגוֹרָא הָדֵין וְסָהֲדָא קָמְתָא אִם אֲנָא לָא אֶעְבַּרʰʰ

---

a Bom. אֲנָא. *b* Bom. בְּנֵי, *A* בְּנַי, *C* בְּנִי. *c* Bom. חֲזִי,
A חֲזִי, *B* חֲזוֹ. *d* Bom. דִּילִי, *B* לִי. *e* Bom. לִבְנָתַי. *f* Bom.
מָה. *g* Bom. לִבְנָתְהֵין (B. לִבְנָתְהֶין). *h* איתא is a better vocalization. *i* Bom. קָיָם. *k* Bom. וִיהֵי. *l* Bom. וּנְסֵיב. *m* Bom.
וְזָקְפַהּ. *n* Bom. וַאֲמַר. *o* B אַבְנֵי. *p* Bom. וַעֲבָדוּ. *q* Bom.
דְגוֹרָא. *r* Bom. וְאָכְלוּ. *s* Bom. וַאֲמַר, *B* has לֵיהּ before יְגַר.
t Bom. דְגוֹרָא. *u* B בֵּינִי. *x* Bom. גַּלְעֵד, *A* גַּלְעָד. *y* Bom.
וְצָפִיתָא. *z* Bom. דַּאֲמַר. *aa* Bom. יִסַּךְ (B. יְסַךְ which is perhaps the best vocalization), *C* יֵסַךְ, *B* יַסַךְ. *bb* Bom. נִתְכַּסֵי.
The best punctuation is נִתְכַּסֵּי. *cc* B תְּעַנֵּה. *dd* Bom. בְּנָתַי
(B. בְּנָתִי). *ee* Bom. אֱנָשׁ. *ff* Bom. קָמָתָא. *gg* Bom. דַּאֲקֵימִית.
The vocalization should be דַּאֲקֵימִית. *hh* Bom. אֵיעֱבַר,
C אֶעְבַּר.

בּוֹלֵךְ יָת דְגוּרָאᵃ הָדֵין וְאִם אֵת לֹא תַעֲבָרᵇ בֵּינִי יָת דְגוּרָאᵃ
הָדֵין וּבֵּית קַמְתָאᶜ הָדָא לְבִישׁוּ

(53) אֱלָהֵיהᵈ דְאַבְרָהָם וֵאלֹהֵיהᵉ דְנָחוֹרᶠ יְדִינוּןᵍ בֵּינָאʰ
אֱלָהָאⁱ דְאַבְהָתְהוֹןᵏ וְקַיֵים יַעֲקֹב בְדַדְחִיל' לֵיהּ אַבוֹהִיᵐ יִצְחָק

(54) וְנָכֵסⁿ יַעֲקֹב נִכְסְתָא בְטוּרָא וּקְרָא לַאֲחוֹהִיᵒ סְמִיכָא
לְחֵמָא וַאֲכַלוּᵖ לַחְמָא וּבָתוּ בְטוּרָא

(55) וְאַקְדִים לָבָן בְצַפְרָא וְנַשִׁיקᵠ לִבְנוֹהִי וְלִבְנָתֵיהּ וּבָרֵיךְʳ
יָתְהוֹןˢ וַאֲזַל' וְתָב" לָבָן לְאַתְרֵיהּ

CHAPTER XLI.

(1) וַהֲוָה מִסוֹף תְרֵין שְׁנִין וּפַרְעֹה חָלֵםˣ וְהָא קָאִיםʸ
עַל נַהֲרָא

(2) וְהָא מִן נַהֲרָא סָלְקָןᶻ שְׁבַעᵃᵃ תוֹרָןᵇᵇ שַׁפִּירָן לְמֶחֱזֵיᶜᶜ
וּפַטִימָן בְסַר וְרָעְיָן בְאַחְוָאᵈᵈ

(3) וְהָא שְׁבַע תּוֹרָן אָחֳרָנָן סָלְקָןᶠᶠ בַתְרֵיהוֹןᵍᵍ מִן נַהֲרָא
בִישָׁן לְמֶחֱזֵי וְחַסִירָןʰʰ בְסַר דְקַמָאⁱⁱ לְקִבְלָתְהוֹן דְתוֹרָתָא עַל
כֵּיף נַהֲרָא

a Bom. דְגוּרָא. *b* C אֵלָב. *c* Bom. קַמְתָא. *d* Bom. אֱלָהֵיהּ.
e Bom. וֵאלָהֵיהּ, C אֱלֹהֵיהּ. *f* Bom. דְנָחוֹר (B. נָחוֹר), A דְיִצְחָק.
g Bom. יְדוּנִין. *h* A בֵּינָא. *i* Bom. אֱלָהֵי. *k* Bom. דְאַבְהָתְהוֹן.
l Bom. בְדַדְחִיל. *m* Bom. אֲבוּהִי. *n* Bom. וּנְכֵיס, B נָכֵיס.
o Bom. לְאַחוֹהִי. *p* Bom. וְאָכְלוּ. *q* Bom. וְנַשִׁיק. *r* Bom. וּבָרֵךְ.
s Bom. יָתְהֵן. *t* Bom. וְאָזַל. *u* Bom. תָב. *x* Bom. חָלִים,
B, C חֲלָם. *y* Bom. קָאֵים. *z* Bom. סָלְקָן. *aa* Bom. שְׁבַע.
bb Bom. תּוֹרִין. *cc* Bom. לְמֶחֱזֵי. *dd* Bom. בְאַחְוָא. *ee* Bom.
אָחֳרָנִין, A אָחֳרָנָן, B אַחֳלָן, C אַחֳלָן. The punctuation should
be אָחֳרָא. *ff* Bom. סָלְקָן which is correct. *gg* Bom. בַתְרֵיהוֹן
(B. has בַתְרֵיהֵן). *hh* Bom. וַחֲסִירָן (B. וְחַסִירָן). *ii* It should
be אָלֵב.

(4) וְאַבָּא̊ תִּוְרְתָא דְּבִרְסָןᵇ לְמֶחֱזֵי וְהֲסִירָן בְּסַר יַת שָׁבַע
תִּוְרָתָא דְּשַׁפִּירָן לְמֶחֱזֵי וּפְטִימָתָאᶜ וְאָתְיָרᵈ פַּרְעֹה
(5) יְדָמֵיךְ וְהֲלַםᵉ שִׁנְיָנוּת וְהָא שָׁבַע שׁוּבְּלִיןᶠ סַלְקָןᵍ בְּקַנְיָאʰ
חַדⁱ פְּטִימָןᵏ וְטָבָן
(6) וְהָא שָׁבַע שׁוּבְּלִין לָקְיָן וּשְׁקִיפָןˡ קִדּוּם צַמְחָןᵐ
בַּתְרֵיהוֹןⁿ
(7) וּבְלִיעָן שׁוּבְּלַיָּא לָקְיָתָא יָת שָׁבַע שׁוּבְּלַיָּא פְּטִימָתָא
וּמַלְיָתָא וְאִתְעַרᵒ פַּרְעֹה וְהָא חֶלְמָאᵖ
(8) וַהֲוָה בְּצַפְרָא וּמִטָרְפָאᵠ רוּחֵיהּ וּשְׁלַח וּקְרָא יָת כָּל
חָרָשֵׁיʳ מִצְרַיִם יָת כָּל חַכִּימָהָאˢ וְאִשְׁתָּעִיᵗ פַּרְעֹה לְהוֹן יָת
חֶלְמֵיהּᵘ וְלֵית דְּפָשַׁרˣ יַתְהוֹןᵡ לְפַרְעֹה
(9) וּמַלִּילʸ רַב שָׁקֵי עִם פַּרְעֹה לְמֵימָר יָת סַרְחָנַיᶻ אֲנָא
מַדְכַּר יוֹמָא דֵין
(10) פַּרְעֹה רְגִיזᵃᵃ עַל עַבְדוֹהִי וִיהַב יָתִי בְּמַטְּרַתᵇᵇ בֵּית
רַב קָטוֹלַיָּא יָתִי וְיָת רַב נַחְתּוֹמֵיᶜᶜ
(11) וַחֲלַמְנָᵈᵈ חֶלְמָᵖ בְּלֵילְיָא חַד אֲנָא וְהוּא גְּבַר כְּפִשְׁרֵ
חֶלְמֵיהּᵖ חֲלַמְנָ
(12) וְתַמָּןᵉᵉ עִמָּנָא עוּלֵים עִבְרָיᶠᶠ עַבְדָּא לְרַב קָטוֹלַיָּא
וְאִשְׁתָּעֵינָאᵍᵍ לֵיהּ וּפָשַׁר לָנָא יָת חֶלְמָנָאʰʰ גְּבַר כְּחֶלְמֵיהּᵖ פָּשַׁר

a Bom. יְאַבָּלָא. *b* Bom. דְּבִרְסָן (B. דְּבִרְשָׁן). *c* Bom. וּפְטִימָתָא.
d A וְאָתִיר. *e* Bom. וְהָלַם. *f* Bom. שׁוּבְלַיָּא. *g* Bom.
סַלְקָן. *h* Bom. בְּקַנְיָא. *i* Bom. חַד. *k* A בְּלִין. *l* Bom.
וּשְׁקִיפָן (B. וּשְׁקִיפָן). *m* Bom. צַמְחַן (B. צַבְחַן). *n* B. בַּתְרֵיהוֹן.
o C וְאָתִיר. *p* Bom. חֶלְפָא and usually S. C חֶלְמָא and
always H. *q* מִטָרְפָא would be a better vocalization.
r Bom. חָרָשֵׁי. *s* חַכִּימָתָא is the correct punctuation. *t* Bom
יְאִשְׁתָּעֵי. *u* C חֶלְמֵיהּ. *x* Bom. דְּפָשַׁר, A דְּפָשֵׁר. *y* Bom. וּמַלִּיל.
z Bom. סִרְחָנֵי (B. סוּרְחָנֵי). *aa* Bom. רְגֵיז. *bb* Bom. בְּמַטְּרַת.
cc Bom. נַחְתּוּמֵי (B. נַחְתּוּמֵי). *dd* Bom. וַחֲלֵמְנָא. *ee* Bom. וְתַמָּן.
(B. וְתַמָּן). *ff* Bom. עִבְרָאָה, A עִבְרָאָ. *gg* Bom. וְאִשְׁתָּעֵינָא.
hh Bom. חֶלְמָנָא but is very inconsistent; thus in verse 11 חֶלְמָא
and חֶלְמֵיהּ and in verse 12 בְּחֶלְמֵיהּ.

(13) וַהֲוָה בְּמָא דְפָשַׁר לָנָא כֵּן הֲוָה וְיָתִי אָתִיב עַל
שִׁמּוּשִׁי וְיָתֵיהּ צְלָב

(14) וּשְׁלַח פַּרְעֹה וּקְרָא יָת יוֹסֵף וְאַרְהֲטוּהִי מִן בֵּית
אֲסִירֵי וְסַפַּר וְשַׁנִּי כְּסוּתֵיהּ וְעַל לְוָת פַּרְעֹה

(15) וַאֲמַר פַּרְעֹה לְיוֹסֵף חֶלְמָא חֲלַמִית וּפָשַׁר לֵית לֵיהּ
וַאֲנָא שְׁמָעִית עֲלָךְ לְמֵימַר דְּאַתְּ שָׁמַע חֶלְמָא וּמְפַשַּׁר יָתֵיהּ

(16) וַאֲתֵיב יוֹסֵף יָת פַּרְעֹה לְמֵימַר לָא מִן חָכְמָתִי אֱלָהִין
מִן קֳ(דָם) יְיָ יְתָתַב שְׁלָמָא דְפַרְעֹה

(17) וּמַלֵּיל פַּרְעֹה עִם יוֹסֵף בְּחֶלְמִי הָאֲנָא קָאִים עַל
כֵּיף נַהֲרָא

(18) וְהָא מִן נַהֲרָא סַלְקָן שְׁבַע תּוֹרָן פְּטִימָן בְּסַר וְשַׁפִּירָן
לְמֶחֱזֵי וְרָעְיָן בְּאַחְוָא

(19) וְהָא שְׁבַע תּוֹרָן אָחֳרָנִין סָלְקָא בַתְרֵיהוֹן חֲסִיכָן
וּבִישָׁן לְמֶחֱזֵי לַחֲדָא וַחֲסִירָן בְּסַר לָא חֲזִיתִי דִכְוָתְהוֹן בְּכָל אַרְעָא
דְמִצְרַיִם לְבִישׁוּ

(20) וַאֲכַלָּא תּוֹרָתָא חֲסִיכָתָא וּבִישָׁתָא יָת שְׁבַע תּוֹרָתָא
קַדְמָיָתָא פְּטִימָתָא

(21) וְעַלָּא לִמְעֵיהוֹן וְלָא אִתְיְדַע אֲרֵי עָלָא לִמְעֵיהוֹן
וּמֶחֱזֵיהוֹן בִּישׁ כִּדְבְקַדְמֵיתָא וְאִתְעָרִית

---

a Bom. דְיִפְשַׁר. *b* Bom. אָתִיב. The best vocalization would be אֲתִיב. *c* Bom. וְאַרְהֲבוּהִי. *d* Bom. חֲלוּמִית. *e* Bom. וּפָשַׁר (B. וּפָשֵׁר). *f* Bom. וּמְפַשֵּׁר, B' יִתְפַשַּׁר. *g* B. יְדָעָה. *h* Bom. יָתִיב. We should expect אֲתִיב. *i* Bom. בְּעֵירִי. *k* Bom. אֱלָהִין. The best vocalization would be אֱלָהֵן. *l* Bom. יְיָתֵב. *m* Bom. יִתְשַׁלְפָּא. *n* Bom. וּמַלִּיל. *o* For an explanation of this word cf. "Aruḥ of Natan b. Jeḥiel". s. v. גב. *q* For the correct vocalization of these two words v. verse 3. *A* אָחֳרָנִין, *B* אַחֲנָא, *C* אֲחֳרָנִין. *r* Bom. חֲסִיכָא. *s* Bom. פְּטִירָא. *t* Bom. יֵעָלָא. *u* Bom. לִמְעֵיהוֹן (B. לְמֵעֵיהֶן). *x* Bom. וּמֶחֱזֵיהֶן (B. וּמֶחֱזֵיהֶן). *y* Bom. כַּד בְּקַדְמֵיתָא.

(22) אֲחָזִיתᵃ בְּחֶלְמִי דְהָא שְׁבַע שִׁבְּלִיןᵇ סָלְקָןᶜ בְּקַנְיָאᵈ חַדᵉ
מַלְיָןⁱ וְטָבָן

(23) וְהָא שְׁבַע שִׁבְּלִין דְקִןʰ לְקִידָןᵍ שְׁקִיפָןⁱ קָדוּםᵏ צַמְחָן
בַּתְרֵיהֹן

(24) וּבָלְעָא שִׁבְּלַיָּא לְקִידַיָּא יָת שְׁבַע שִׁבְּלַיָּאˡ
וַאֲמָרִיתᵐ לְחָרָשַׁיָּאⁿ וְלֵית דִּמְחַוֵּי לִי

(25) וַאֲמַרᵒ יוֹסֵף לְפַרְעֹה חֶלְמָא דְפַרְעֹה חַד הוּא יָת דִּי
עָתִידᵖ לְמֶעְבַּד קֳדָם יְיָ חַוִּי לְפַרְעֹה

(26) שְׁבַע תּוֹרָתָא טָבָתָא שְׁבַע שְׁנַיָּאⁱ אִינוּן וּשְׁבַע שִׁבְּלַיָּא
טָבָתָא שְׁבַע שְׁנַיָּא אִינוּןⁱ חֶלְמָא חַד הוּא

(27) וּשְׁבַע תּוֹרָתָא חֲסִידָתָא וּבִישָׁתָא דְסָלְקָןˢ בַּתְרֵיהֹן
שְׁבַע שְׁנַיָּאⁱ אִינוּן וּשְׁבַע שִׁבְּלַיָּא לְקִידָתָא דִּשְׁקִיפָן קָדוּם יְהֶוְיָןᵘ
שְׁבַע שְׁנֵי

(28) הוּא פִּתְגָמָא דְמַלֵּלִיתˣ עִם פַּרְעֹהʸ דִּי עָתִידⁱ לְמֶעְבַּד
אַחְזִיᶻᵃ יָת פַּרְעֹהᵇᵇ

(29) הָא שְׁבַע שְׁנַיָּא אָתְיָן סַבְעָא רַבָּא בְּכָל אַרְעָא
דְמִצְרָיִם

(30) וִיקוּמָןᶜᶜ שְׁבַע שְׁנֵי כָפְנָא בַּתְרֵיהוֹן וְיִתְנְשֵׁי כָּל
סַבְעָאᵈᵈ בְּאַרְעָא דְמִצְרַיִם וִישֵׁיצֵי כַּפְנָא יָת עַמָּא דְאַרְעָאᵉᵉ

(31) וְלָא יִתְיְדַע סַבְעָאᶠᶠ בְּאַרְעָא מִן קֳדָם כַּפְנָא הַהוּא
דִּיהֵי בָתַר כֵּן אֲרֵי תַקִּיףᵍᵍ הוּא לַחֲדָא

---

a Bom. אַחֲזִית. *b* Bom. שִׁבְּלִין. *c* Bom. סָלְקִין. *d* Bom. בְּקַנְיָא. *e* Bom. חַד. *f* Bom. מַלְיָן. *g* Bom. וְגַן. *h* Bom. דִקְיָן. *i* Bom. שְׁקִידָן. *k* Bom. קְדִים (B. נַצְבָן). *l* אִבְאָ. *m* Bom. וַאֲמָרָה. *n* Bom. לְחַרְשַׁיָּא. *o* Bom. וַאֲמַר. *p* A עָתִיד. *q* Bom. לְמֶעְבַּד. *r* Bom. אֵינוּן so *B* and *C* אִנּוּן. *s* See verse 3. *t* Bom. שְׁנֵי. *u* Bom. יְהֶוְיָן. *x* Bom. דִּי מַלֵּלִית. *y* *B* inserts יָת before פַרְעֹה. *z* *B* חֲזִי. *aa* Bom. אַחְזֵי. *bb* *A* (omitting יָת). *cc* Bom. וִיקוּמִין (B. וִיקוּמוּן), *C* יְקוּמָן. *dd* Bom. שַׂבְעָא. *ee* *B* (text) אַרְעָא דְּ— but margin as above עַמָּא דְאַרְעָא. *ff* Bom. שַׂבְעָא. *gg* Bom. תַּקִּיף (B. תְקִיף).

(32) וְעַל דְּאַנּוּןᵃ הֲלָמָא בְּפַרְעֹה תַּרְתֵּין זִמְנִין אֲרֵי תְקֵןᵇ פִּתְגָּמָא מִן קֳ(דָם) יְיָ וּמוֹחֵיᶜ יְיָ לְמֶעְבְּדֵיהּᵈ

(33) וּכְעַן יֶחְזֵיᵉ פַּרְעֹה גְּבַר סֻכְלְתָןᶠ חַכִּים וִישַׁוִּנֵּיהּᵍ עַל אַרְעָא דְמִצְרָיִם

(34) יַעֲבֵידʰ פַּרְעֹה וִימַנֵּי מְהֵימְנִין עַל אַרְעָא וִיזָרֵז יָת אַרְעָא דְמִצְרַיִם בְּשֶׁבַע שְׁנֵי שַׂבְעָאⁱ

(35) וְיִכְנְשׁוּןᵏ יָת כָּל עֲבוּרˡ שְׁנַיָּא טָבָתָא דְאָתְיָן אִלֵּיןᵐ וְיִצְבְּרוּןⁿ עֲבוּרָא תְּחוֹת יְדᵒ מְהֵימְנֵי פַרְעֹהᵖ עֲבוּרָא בְּקִרְוַיָּא וְיִטְּרוּן

(36) וִיהֵיᵍ עֲבוּרָא גְּנִיזʳ בְּעַמָּא דְאַרְעָא לְשֶׁבַע שְׁנֵי כַּפְנָא דִיהוֹיָןˢ בְּאַרְעָא דְמִצְרַיִם וְלָא יִשְׁתֵּיצֵיᵗ עַמָּא דְאַרְעָא בְּכַפְנָא

(37) וּשְׁפַר פִּתְגָּמָא בְּעֵינֵי פַרְעֹה וּבְעֵינֵי כָּל עַבְדוֹהִי

(38) וַאֲמַר פַּרְעֹה לְעַבְדוֹהִי הֲנִשְׁכַּחᵘ כְּדֵין גְּבַר דְּרוּחַˣ נְבוּאָה מִן קֳ(דָם) יְיָ בֵּיהּ

(39) וַאֲמַר פַּרְעֹה לְיוֹסֵף בָּתַר דְּהוֹדַע יְיָ יָתָךְ יָת כָּל דָּאʸ לֵית סֻכְלְתָןˢ וְחַכִּים כְּוָתָךְ

(40) אַתְּ תְּהֵי מְמֻנָּאᵃᵃ עַל בֵּיתִי וְעַל מֵימְרָךְ יִתְזַן כָּל עַמִּי לְחוֹד כֻּרְסֵי מַלְכוּתָא הָדֵין אֵיחוֹרᵇᵇ לְקִיר מִנָּךְ

(41) וַאֲמַר פַּרְעֹה לְיוֹסֵף חֲזִיᶜᶜ דְּמַנֵּיתִי יָתָךְ עַל כָּל אַרְעָא דְמִצְרָיִם

(42) וְאַעְדִּיᵈᵈ פַּרְעֹה יָת עִזְקָתֵיהּᵉᵉ מֵעַל יְדֵיהּ וִיהַב יָתַהּᶠᶠ

a Bom. דְּאַרְגֵּז, B דָּאָגֵי. It should be דְּאָגֵי. *b* Bom. תְּקֵין. *c* וּמְיַחֵי is the correct punctuation. *d* Bom. לְמֶעְבְּדֵיהּ. *e* Bom. יֶחֱזֵי. *f* Bom. סֻכְלְתָן. *g* Bom. וִימַנִּינֵיהּ. *h* Bom. יַעֲבֵיד (B. יַעֲבֵיד). *i* Bom. שַׂבְעָא. *k* Bom. וְיִכְנְשׁוּן. *l* C עֲבוּרָא. *m* Bom. הָאִלֵּין. *n* Bom. וְיִצְבְּרוּן. *o* Bom. יְדָא. *p* Bom. דְפַרְעֹה. *q* Bom. יְהֵי. *r* A גָנִיז. *s* Bom. דֶּהֱוָיָן, C דִּיהוֹיָן. *t* B יִשְׁתֵּיצֵי. *u* Bom. הֲנִשְׁכַּח, A הֲנַשְׁכַּח. *x* Bom. דְּרוּחַ. *y* Bom. דָּא. *z* Bom. סֻכְלְתָן (B. דְּסֻכְלְתָן), B, C דְּסֻכְלְתָן. *aa* A יְהֵא. *bb* Bom. אֱהֵא. *cc* Bom. חֲזִי. *dd* A וְאַעְדִּי. *ee* Bom. עִזְקָתֵיהּ, A עִזְקָתֵיהּ, B עִזְקְתֵיהּ (?). *ff* Bom. יָדֵיהּ.

עַל יְדָא דְיוֹסֵף ᵃוְאַלְבֵּישׁ יָתֵיהּ לְבוּשִׁין דְבוּץ וְשַׁוִי מְנִכָא
דְדַהֲבָא עַל צַוְארֵיהּ

(43) ᵇוְאַרְכֵּיב יָתֵיהּ בִּרְתִיכָא ᶜתִנְיֵתָא ᵈדִילֵיהּ ᵉוְאַכְרִיזוּ
קֳדָמוֹהִי דֵין אַבָּא לְמַלְכָּא וּמַנֵי יָתֵיהּ עַל כָּל אַרְעָא דְמִצְרָיִם

(44) וַאֲמַר פַּרְעֹה לְיוֹסֵף אֲנָא פַרְעֹה ᶠיְבַר מֵימְרָךְ לָא
יָרִים ᵍגְבַר יַת יְדֵיהּ לְמֵיחַד זֵין ʰיָת רַגְלֵיהּ לְמִרְכַּב עַל ⁱסוּסְיָא
בְּכָל אַרְעָא דְמִצְרָיִם

(45) ᵏוּקְרָא פַרְעֹה שׁוּם יוֹסֵף גַבְרָא דְמִטַּמְרָן ˡגַּלְיָן ᵐלֵיהּ ⁿ
וִיהַב לֵיהּ יָת אָסְנַת בַּת פּוֹטִי פֶרַע רַבָּא דְאוֹן ᵒלְאִתּוּ וּנְפַק יוֹסֵף
שַׁלִיט עַל ᵖכָּל אַרְעָא דְמִצְרָיִם

(46) וְיוֹסֵף בַּר תְּלָתִין שְׁנִין כַּד קָם (קְדָם) פַּרְעֹה מַלְכָּא
דְמִצְרַיִם וּנְפַק יוֹסֵף מִן (קְדָם) פַּרְעֹה וְעָבַר בְּכָל אַרְעָא דְמִצְרָיִם

(47) וּכְנָשַׁת ᵠאַרְעָא בִּשְׁבַע שְׁנֵי שׂבעא ʳעֲבוּרָא
לְאוֹצָרִין ˢ

(48) וּכְנַשׁ יָת כָּל עֲבוּר שְׁבַע שְׁנַיָא דַהֲוָאָה בְּאַרְעָא דְמִצְרָיִם
וִיהַב עִבּוּרָא בְּקִרְוַיָא עִבּוּר חֲקַל קַרְתָּא ᵘדִבְסַחֲרָנָהָא ˣיְהַב בְּגַוָהּ

(49) וּכְנַשׁ יוֹסֵף עִבּוּרָא כְחָלָא דְיַמָא סַגִי לַחֲדָא עַד דְפַסְקוּ ʸ
לְמִמְנֵי ᶻאֲרֵי לֵית מִנְיָן

(50) וּלְיוֹסֵף ᵃᵃאִתְיְלִידוּ תְּרֵין בְּנִין עַד לָא עָלַת ᵇᵇשְׁתָּא
דְכַפְנָא ᶜᶜדִילֵידַת לֵיהּ אָסְנַת בַּת פּוֹטִי פֶרַע רַבָּא דְאוֹן

---

a Bom. גִּנְדְּבָא. *b* Bom. וְאַרְכֵּיב. *c* Bom. תִּנְיָנָא. *d* Bom. דִי לֵיהּ. *e* Bom. וַעֲנֵי. *f* בַּר would be a better vocalization. *g* *A* יְרִים. *h* Bom. וְיָת. *i* Bom. סוּסְיָא. *k* Should it be שֵׁם? *l* Bom. דְּגִשְׁשִׁין (B. דְּנִישְׁיָן). Cf. Winer: De Onkeloso eiusque Paraphrasi Chaldaica: Leipzig 1820. p. 28. *m* Bom. יַתֵּיהּ. *n* Instead of גַּלְיָן לֵיהּ דְמִטַּמְרָן גַבְרָא, *C* simply has פָּשַׁר חֶלְמַיָא which is perhaps preferable. *o* Bom. לְאִנְתּוּ. *p* *A* has בְּכָל instead of כָּל. *q* Bom. דְיָהֵב. *r* Bom. עֲבוּרָא. *s* Bom. בְּאוֹצְרֵי. *t* *C* לְמִצָלֵי. *u* Bom. דְקַרְתָּא. *x* Bom. דְּבִסְחַרְנָהָא. *y* Bom. דְפָסַק. *z* Bom. לְמִמְנֵי. *aa* *C* אִתְיַלְדָן. *bb* Bom. עָלַת. *cc* Bom. דִי לִידַת.

G

(51) וּקְרָא יוֹסֵף יָת שׁוֹם בּוּכְרָא מְנַשֶּׁה אֲרֵי אַנְשְׁיַנִי" יְיָ יָת כָּל עַמְלִי[b] וְיָת כָּל בֵּית אַבָּא

(52) וְיָת שׁוֹם תִּנְיָנָא[c] קְרָא אֶפְרָיִם[d] אֲרֵי אַפְשַׁנִי יְיָ בְּאַרְעָא[e] שִׁעבּוּדִי

(53) וּשְׁלִימָא שְׁבַע שְׁנֵי שִׂבְעָא דַּהֲוָאָה בְּאַרְעָא דְמִצְרָיִם

(54) וְשָׁרִיאָה[f] שְׁבַע שְׁנֵי כַפְנָא לְמֵיתֵי כְּמָא דַּאֲמַר[g] יוֹסֵף וַהֲוָה כַפְנָא בְּכָל אַרְעָתָא וּבְכָל אַרְעָא דְמִצְרַיִם הֲוָה לַחְמָא

(55) וּכְפֵינַת[h] כָּל אַרְעָא דְמִצְרַיִם וּצְוַח[i] עַמָּא קֳ(דָם) פַּרְעֹה לְלַחְמָא[k] וַאֲמַר פַּרְעֹה לְכָל מִצְרָאֵי אִיזִילוּ לְוַת יוֹסֵף דְּיֵמַר[l] לְכוֹן תַּעַבְדוּן[n]

(56) וְכַפְנָא הֲוָה עַל כָּל אַפֵּי אַרְעָא וּפְתַח יוֹסֵף יָת כָּל אוֹצְרַיָּא[o] דִּבְהוֹן[p] עֲבוּרָא וְזַבִּין[q] לְמִצְרָיִם[r] וּתְקֵיף כַּפְנָא בְּאַרְעָא דְמִצְרַיִם

(57) וְכָל דַיְירֵי[s] אַרְעָא אֲתוֹ[t] לְמִצְרַיִם לְמִזְבַּן עֲבוּרָא מִן יוֹסֵף אֲרֵי תְקֵיף[u] כַּפְנָא בְּכָל אַרְעָא

---

a Bom. אַנְשְׁיָנִי, *B* אַנְשַׁלִי. *b* Bom. עֲמָלִי, *B* עֲמַל. *c* *A* תִּנְיָיקָא.
d *A* אֶפְרַיִם. *e* Bom. בְּאַרְעָא. *f* Bom. וּשְׁרִיאָה. *g* Bom. אֲמַר.
h Bom. וּכְפִינַת. *i* Bom. צְוַח. *k* *B*, *C* כָּל לַחְמָא. *l* *A* דְּיֵמַר.
m Bom. דְּיֵיְמַר. *n* Bom. תַּעְבְּדוּן (B. תַּעַבְדוּן). *o* Bom. אוֹצְרַיָּא.
p Bom. דִּי בְהוֹן. *q* Bom. וְזָבִין. *r* Bom. לְמִצְרָאֵי (B. לְמִצְרָאֵי).
s Bom. דַיָּירֵי. *t* Bom. אֲתוֹ. *u* Bom. תְּקֵיף.

ADDENDA ET CORRIGENDA.

An italic number signifies that the line is counted from the bottom of the page upwards.

Page 3, line 5. Cf. Zunz, l. c. p. 132.
„ 6, „ ult. Pro he lege the.
„ 8, „ 7. Cf. Seligsohn. l. c. p. 20.
„ 13, „ 17. Pro devise lege device.
„ 13, „ 2. Pro S. lege Š.
„ 15, „ 3. Cf. Diwan of Jehudah Hallevi; No. 65 in Luzzatto's Edition where יֹאמַר (it should be יֹאמַר) is rimed with הָמָר.
„ 15, „ 6. Pro קָהֵל lege קָהָל.
„ 16, „ 4. Cf. Friedländer. "A third system of symbols for the Hebrew vowels and accents". (Jewish Quarterly Review VII, 27. p. 567),
„ 16, „ 2. Pro exemples lege examples.
„ 19, „ 2. Pro הֹשַׁלְבִין lege הֹשַׁלְבִין.
„ 21, „ 6. Cf. אֱלִיל יְתֵרֹתִי (Jeremiah 14, 14) and שֵׁרִיתְךָ (Jeremiah 15, 11).
„ 26, „ 2. Pro כְּרֵסָא lege כָּרְסָא.
„ 32, „ 7. Cf. Aboth de R. Nathan. Ch. 34.
„ 37, „ 12. Cf. Raši a. l.
„ 46, „ 9. קָרִים lege קָרִים.
„ 47, „ 15. שָׁוֵה lege שָׁוֶה.
„ 47, „ 2. Cf. Barth in ZDMG. XXX, p. 193.
„ 48, „ 2. Pro שְׁלַם lege שְׁלַם.
„ 50, „ 4. Cf. Midraš Genesis Rabba ch. 42. § 7 in Wilna Edition.

Page 50, line 12. Pro הַשְּׁבִּיִן lege הַשְּׁבִּין.
" 51, " 8. שְׁבִיאָ lege שְׁבִיאָ.
" 52, " 1. Pro סְרִיר lege סְרִיר.
" 56. " 11. Pro שְׁבִיבִין lege שְׁבִיבִין.
" 56, " 5. Pro הִהַ lege הִהַ.
" 58, " 6. Pro יְאִשְׁוִר lege יְאִשְׁוִר.
" 59, " 6. Pro הַבֵאָ lege הַבֵאָ.
" 59, " 13. Pro חָיְדְיִתִין lege חָיְדְיִתִין.
" 60, " 5. v. Ibn Ezra, to this verse, who explains the Jewish Interpretation from צפן = to hide and کشف = to open.
" 61, " 10. Pro הַשָּׁה lege הַשָּׁה.
" 62, " 2. Pro הַלָּה et הַשָּׁ lege הַלָּה et הַשָּׁ.
" 63, " ult. v. Barth in ZDMG. XXX. p. 192.
" 64, " 7. " " " " " p. 190.
" 67, " 3. v. Seligsohn. l. c. p. 26.
" 71, " 11. Pro יִרְצַק lege יִרְצַק.
" 73, " 1. Pro דָאָ lege דָאָ.
" 78, " 9. Vide Friedländer. l. c. p. 568.

A few Ḥireqs which sprung off during printing are not specified as they are easily recognisable.

www.ingramcontent.com/pod-product-compliance
Lightning Source LLC
Chambersburg PA
CBHW020146170426
43199CB00010B/914